NEGOTIATING

Comprehensive Lar

MW01104663

Negotiating the Deal provides the first systematic and comprehensive analysis of the factors that explain both completed and incomplete treaty negotiations between Aboriginal groups and the federal, provincial, and territorial governments of Canada. Since 1973, groups that have never signed treaties with the Crown have been invited to negotiate what the government calls "comprehensive land claims agreements," otherwise known as modern treaties, which formally transfer jurisdiction, ownership, and title over selected lands to Aboriginal signatories. Despite their importance, not all groups have completed such agreements – a situation that is problematic not only for governments but for Aboriginal groups interested in rebuilding their communities and economies.

Using in-depth interviews with Indigenous, federal, provincial, and territorial officials, Christopher Alcantara compares the experiences of four Aboriginal groups: the Kwanlin Dün First Nation (with a completed treaty) and the Kaska Nations (with incomplete negotiations) in Yukon Territory, and the Inuit (completed) and Innu (incomplete) in Newfoundland and Labrador. Based on the experiences of these groups, Alcantara argues that scholars and policymakers need to pay greater attention to the institutional framework governing treaty negotiations and, most importantly, to the active role that Aboriginal groups play in these processes.

CHRISTOPHER ALCANTARA is an associate professor in the Department of Political Science at Wilfrid Laurier University.

Negotiating the Deal

Comprehensive Land Claims Agreements in Canada

CHRISTOPHER ALCANTARA

UNIVERSITY OF TORONTO PRESS
Toronto Buffalo London

© University of Toronto Press 2013
Toronto Buffalo London
www.utppublishing.com
Printed in the U.S.A.

ISBN 978-1-4426-4477-9 (cloth)
ISBN 978-1-4426-1284-6 (paper)

Printed on acid-free, 100% post-consumer recycled paper.

Library and Archives Canada Cataloguing in Publication

Alcantara, Christopher, 1978–
Negotiating the deal : comprehensive land claims agreements in Canada /
Christopher Alcantara.

Includes bibliographical references and index.
ISBN 978-1-4426-4477-9 (bound). – ISBN 978-1-4426-1284-6 (pbk.)

1. Native peoples – Canada – Claims.   2. Native peoples – Canada – Government relations.   3. Native peoples – Land tenure – Canada.   I. Title.

KE7718.A78 2013   346.7104'3208997   C2012-908144-2
KF8208.A932 2013

This book has been published with the help of a grant from the Canadian
Federation for the Humanities and Social Sciences, through the Awards to
Scholarly Publications Program, using funds provided by the Social Sci-
ences and Humanities Research Council of Canada.

University of Toronto Press acknowledges the financial assistance to its
publishing program of the Canada Council for the Arts and the Ontario
Arts Council.

University of Toronto Press acknowledges the financial support of the
Government of Canada through the Canada Book Fund for its publishing
activities.

For Kerry Lee, Kees, Adelaide, and Anthony

Contents

Illustrations

Maps

Tables

Acknowledgments

I am grateful to many people for helping me complete this book. First and foremost, this book benefited immensely from discussions with officials from the federal government, the Newfoundland and Labrador government, the Yukon government, the Nunatsiavut government, the Labrador Innu, the Kwanlin Dün First Nation, and the Kaska Nations. In particular, I want to acknowledge the help of Tim Koepke, Dermot Flynn, Veryan Haysom, Anne King, Ray Hawco, Bob Pelley, Ruby Carter, Dave Porter, Steve Walsh, Hammond Dick, Liard McMillan, Eileen Van Bibber, Scott Serson, Tom Beaudoin, Jim Mackenzie, and Chesley Anderson, all of whom were especially helpful in answering my many questions.

This book benefited greatly from discussions with Graham White, Grace Skogstad, and Peter Russell at the University of Toronto, as well as Frances Abele (Carleton University) and Doug McArthur (SFU). All of these individuals were extremely patient, helpful, and rigorous with their advice throughout the research and writing process. Much of their input guided the initial specification of my analysis and arguments.

This research was supported by a number of programs and scholarships, including the Ontario Graduate Scholarship Program, the Institute for Humane Studies Fellowship, the Liberty Fund, the Northern Scientific Training Program, and the Labrador Institute in Happy Valley–Goose Bay. Research in the Canadian north is extremely expensive and these programs and scholarships were crucial in helping me complete this book.

In terms of bringing this book to publication, Daniel Quinlan, acquisitions editor at University of Toronto Press, was instrumental. I've never met a more helpful, savvy, and supportive editor than Daniel, who not only fielded my many emails and queries, but also expertly guided my manuscript through the intricacies of the review and publication process. I also want to thank the five reviewers at UTP who read this manuscript at various stages. Although at times they disagreed vigorously with me and, indirectly, with each other, their input and debate helped strengthen and sharpen the final arguments put forward here. This book has been published with the help of a grant from the Canadian Federation for the Humanities and Social Sciences, through the Awards to Scholarly Publications Program, using funds provided by the Social Sciences and Humanities Research Council of Canada.

My wife, Kerry Lee Hunt, and my children, Kees Rafael Alcantara, Adelaide Aleeden Alcantara, and Anthony John Birks Alcantara, were crucial throughout this process. A book requires a significant amount of sacrifice from immediate family members and they shouldered this sacrifice without complaint. Rafael and Eden Alcantara, my parents, have also been important to the success of this project, as have the support of Tony and Carmen Hidalgo, Gerry and Tessie Suarez, Josefa and Flaviano Sagun, Christopher Cochrane, Jen Nelles, Amardeep "Watch out for that van" Athwal, David Chandonnet, and Tom Flanagan.

Finally, I would like to thank Cambridge University Press for granting me permission to use material from my articles "Explaining Aboriginal Treaty Negotiation Outcomes in Canada: The Cases of the Inuit and the Innu in Labrador," *Canadian Journal of Political Science* 40:1 (March 2007): 185–207, and "Claiming the City: Co-Operation and Making the Deal in Urban Comprehensive Land Claims Negotiations in Canada," *Canadian Journal of Political Science* 40:1 (September 2009): 705–28; and Oxford University Press for granting me permission to use material from my article "To Treaty or Not to Treaty? Aboriginal Peoples and Comprehensive Land Claims Negotiations in Canada," *Publius: Journal of Federalism* 38:2 (Spring 2008): 343–69. Maps 2.1 and 3.1 were reproduced with the permission of Natural Resources Canada 2011, courtesy of the Atlas of Canada. Map 3.2 was reproduced with the permission of the Yukon Department of Environment. Maps 2.2 and 2.3 were reproduced with the permission of the Government of Newfoundland and Labrador and the (US) National Museum of Natural History respectively.

NEGOTIATING THE DEAL

Comprehensive Land Claims Agreements in Canada

Introduction

In 1973, the Supreme Court of Canada in R. v. Calder rendered a legal decision that would have significant consequences for Aboriginal and non-Aboriginal peoples in Canada. In that decision, a majority of the court for the first time recognized the legal existence of "Aboriginal title to land" (Macklem, 2001: 268–9). As a result, "the federal government was forced to reconsider at least some elements of its policy on land claims because of Calder, a decision that confirmed that Indian title is a valid right in common law" (RCAP, 1996: 533; see also Macklem, 2001: 269). Reflecting on the court's decision, Prime Minister Pierre Trudeau remarked that "perhaps you had more legal rights than we thought when we did the White Paper" (quoted in Asch, 1999: 432).[1]

Later that year, the federal government responded to this legal decision by inviting Aboriginal groups to file what it called comprehensive land claims (CLC; Scholtz, 2006). Under this process, Aboriginal groups that had never signed treaties with the federal government but had a valid claim to their traditional lands could negotiate with the Crown to complete a modern treaty. A typical comprehensive land claims settlement could include large amounts of land and money, and jurisdiction over natural resources, fish and wildlife, migratory birds, taxation, economic development, land use planning, heritage, water management, and other far-reaching jurisdictions. Sometimes, these settlements include self-government provisions. For the federal, provincial, and territorial governments of Canada, comprehensive land claims agreements are important tools for establishing certainty. In their view, a modern treaty replaces what government actors see as undefined and highly ambiguous Aboriginal rights with specific, defined treaty rights and title. For Aboriginal peoples, by contrast, comprehensive land claims agreements are mechanisms to affirm and protect their traditional landholdings and territories.

Shortly after the federal government opened up the comprehensive land claims process, a number of Aboriginal groups took up the federal government's offer and filed claims.[2] Among those initial groups were the Kwanlin Dün First Nation (KDFN) and the Kaska Nations in the Yukon Territory, and later the Inuit and Innu in Labrador. Surprisingly, despite filing their land claims at approximately the same time, only the KDFN and the Labrador Inuit were able to complete treaties.

The central question of this book is the following: Why were the KDFN and the Labrador Inuit able to complete comprehensive land claims agreements and why were the Kaska Nations and the Labrador Innu not able to complete them? Surprisingly, despite the practical and scholarly importance of this question, there is no consensus as to why some groups have been able to achieve settlements and why others have not.[3] Instead, students of modern treaties have tended to study single cases in great detail, which unfortunately limits the transferability of their findings to other cases, or they have engaged in purely theoretical inquiries, with no systematic empirical work to test their theories.

As a result, a diverse set of explanations has emerged. One set of studies, for instance, examines the James Bay treaty experience in the early to mid-1970s and finds that the presence of a major resource development opportunity on Aboriginal lands is a key factor for producing a treaty settlement. (Rynard, 2001; Feit, 1980; Diamond, 1985). Another view is that the Crown itself is a major obstacle to treaty settlements. These scholars suggest that shifts in federal negotiation policy have affected the pace at which settlements have been produced (Abele, Graham, and Maslove, 2000; Alcantara, 2009). Former Yukon premier and negotiator Tony Penikett (2006) builds on this point by arguing that the British Columbia treaty process in particular has failed to produce many completed treaties because government actors have tended to have inflexible political mandates, have lacked political will, or have failed to provide sufficient incentives for professional negotiators to complete agreements quickly (see also Widdowson and Howard, 2008: chap. 3; de Costa, 2003).

Others suggest that the Crown's historical interference in Aboriginal societies has significantly hindered the ability of Aboriginal groups to complete settlements.[4] Specifically, state actions like the resettlement of Aboriginal peoples, the creation of band council governments, and the under funding of Aboriginal communities hamper the ability of Aboriginal groups to marshal the necessary resources to complete treaties. As well, state interference can play havoc with the internal dynamics of Aboriginal groups. For instance, the Labrador Innu were underfunded and relocated several times during the twentieth century, leading to severe socio-economic distress and political infighting. As a result, the Innu have struggled to marshal the necessary resources and community support to complete a treaty.

Others point to differences between non-Aboriginal and Aboriginal actors as being important obstacles to treaty settlements. Abele and Prince (2003: 150–1), for instance, argue that federal and provincial governments see themselves as "representatives of the Crown meeting with minorities within Canada," whereas Aboriginal peoples see themselves as nations negotiating with Canada as equals. This difference prevents the two sides from achieving agreement on crucial issues such as self-government, land selection, ownership and management of resources, and certainty and finality (Tully 2001).

Finally, some suggest that "cultural match" explains settlements and non-settlements. These authors argue that some Indigenous cultures may be more compatible with Canadian culture than others, making it easier for them to complete modern treaties (see Kulchyski, 2005; Nadasdy, 2003). These cultural attributes may be inherent to the Aboriginal groups themselves, or they may have developed over time through contact with colonial actors and societies. Regardless, cultural match could make it easier for some groups, like the Inuit who negotiated the creation of Nunavut, to complete modern treaties with the Canadian state (McPherson, 2003).

Explaining Settlements and Non-Settlements: A Framework for Analysis

So what explains variation in modern treaty settlements and non-settlements in Canada? Based on the theoretical assumptions of rational-choice institutionalism and the experiences of four Aboriginal groups in Canada, this book argues that variation in negotiation outcomes can be best explained by taking into account the preferences, incentives, and strategies of the negotiating parties, all of which are influenced by the institutional framework governing the comprehensive land claims process. Rather than adopting an inductive approach, this book takes a deductive approach by applying a rational-choice institutional framework to the task of explaining variation in modern treaty settlements versus non-settlements (see North, 1990; Hall and Taylor, 1996). A rational-choice institutional framework is useful for theorizing about modern treaty settlements and non-settlements because treaty negotiations are essentially bargaining situations in which government and Aboriginal actors seek to negotiate treaties that maximize their preferences (goals).[5] Although "thin-rationalists" argue that the contents of preferences do not matter (hence preferences are "thin"), "thick-rationalists" argue that they do matter (and hence are "thick") (Shapiro and Green, 1996: 17–19). They matter because if the contents of the preferences of the actors are similar, then an agreement may be easier to achieve. If actors have different preferences, then an agreement may be more difficult to achieve. Preferences tend not to be perfectly aligned. Rather, what matters is the distance between preferences (see Simeon, 2006: 14–15; Tsebelis, 2002).

In addition to preferences, actors are subject to incentives (opportunities and constraints) that organize their strategic interactions with each other. Incentives determine whether the negotiating actors should work towards or against completed agreements. These incentives are generated by the relevant institutional structures under which the actors negotiate (North, 1990). Government and Aboriginal actors in the comprehensive land claims process will interact with each other according to their preferences and their positions within the existing institutional context. The institutional context, however, does not predetermine political outcomes (Encarnacion, 2000: 486). Rather, it determines the range of possible outcomes and the likelihood that such outcomes will obtain, given the preferences that actors bring to the process. In the words of Knill and Lenschow (2001), "Institutions are conceived as an opportunity structure that constrains and enables the behavior of self-interested actors. Institutions limit the range of strategic options that are available to actors, however – in contrast to structure-based approaches – without entirely prestructuring political decisions towards certain outcomes" (Knill and Lenschow, 2001: 195; see also Shepsle, 1989).

The institutional context is also important for shaping the power relations between the negotiating actors. Power relations matter because the relative power of the actors can greatly affect variation in outcomes (see Macklem, 2001: 96). Gerardo Munck (1994) makes a similar observation: "To say actors have choices does not mean that outcomes are random or that actors are equally likely to pick any set of potential institutional designs. Probably the primary factor explaining the shape of emerging institutions, as has been underlined by various authors, is the *relative power* of the actors involved in the process, the rulers and the opposition" (emphasis added) (Munck, 1994: 370). In the case of comprehensive land claims negotiations, the outcomes will be influenced by the power relations between the governments, on the one hand, and the negotiating Aboriginal groups, on the other (Macklem, 2001: 96). If the power relations are not balanced, then the outcomes will very much depend on the ability of the weaker actors to influence the stronger actors, assuming their preferences are different (see, for instance, Rueschemeyer, Stephens, and Stephens, 1992; Tsebelis, 2002). Power relations are affected by the distribution of "political resources." Different actors have varying amounts of political resources that they can use to influence each other (Simeon, 2006: 15).

In comprehensive land claims negotiations, as will be shown in subsequent chapters, the federal, provincial, and territorial governments are the dominant actors[6] and benefit greatly from the status quo, wherein treaty completion is delayed for as long as possible. The Aboriginal actors, by contrast, are much weaker in terms of the resources that they can bring to bear against the Crown. They also want to complete treaties quickly, since doing so gives them a number of significant powers and resources that are much greater than what they currently enjoy under the status quo. To complete treaties, therefore, requires the Aboriginal groups (the weaker actors) to convince the federal, provincial, and territorial governments (the dominant actors) that completing treaties is in their interests. They must do so because the government actors are the "veto players," defined by George Tsebelis (2002: 19) as the "individual or collective actors whose agreement is necessary for a change of the status quo."

The ability of the Aboriginal groups to convince the veto players to complete settlement agreements, however, is conditioned heavily by the institutional framework, Aboriginal cultural legacies, and Aboriginal historical interactions with the Canadian state. As Paul Nadasdy (2003: 5), for instance, argues:

> If Aboriginal peoples wish to participate in co-management, land claims negotiations, and other processes that go along with this new relationship, then they must engage in dialogue with wildlife biologists, lawyers, and other government officials. First Nations peoples can of course speak to these officials any way they want, but if they wish to be taken seriously,

then their linguistic utterances must conform to the very particular forms and formalities of the official linguistic fields of wildlife management, Canadian property law, and so forth. Only through years of schooling or informal training can First Nations people become fluent in the social and linguistic conventions of these official discourses. Those who do not do so are effectively barred from participation in these processes.

To be successful in treaty negotiations requires Aboriginal groups to adopt the official discourse, to negotiate only those issues that the governments want to negotiate, to avoid confrontation, and to acquire particular types of expertise to skilfully navigate the negotiation process.

Historical and cultural legacies enter into the analytical framework as conditioning influences that affect the likelihood of different Aboriginal groups adopting the goals, behaviours, and strategies that government actors require to complete treaties. Some Aboriginal cultures, for instance, may be more compatible with the cultural norms of the Canadian government than others, thus affecting the likelihood of certain outcomes. As mentioned above, McPherson (2003) argues that the compatibility of Inuit and Canadian political cultures helped facilitate the completion of the Nunavut Land Claims Agreement in 1993. In addition to cultural match, historical interactions between Aboriginal groups and the Canadian state may affect the propensity of the Aboriginal groups to adopt the necessary strategies for completing a treaty (Kulchyski, 2005; Nadasdy, 2003). In the case of the Labrador Innu, for instance, the Canadian state underfunded and relocated the Innu several times, which in turn generated significant social, economic, and political problems that hindered the group's ability to complete a treaty. Yet such historical, cultural, and institutional constraints do not completely predetermine Aboriginal choices and outcomes. In the empirical chapters to follow, I will show that Aboriginal leaders can give their groups *some* agency in the way that they choose to respond to the requirements of the dominant government actors. Leaders can engage in certain types of strategies that can alter somewhat the effect of historical, cultural, and institutional constraints. This argument is consistent with the theoretical structure-agency arguments made by scholars such as Encarnacion (2000) and Knill and Lenschow (2001).

In sum, theory suggests that government and Aboriginal actors come to the negotiating table with a set of preferences and incentives regarding the CLC negotiation process. The distance between Aboriginal and government preferences and the nature of the relevant institutional framework greatly influence their interactions. The main task of Aboriginal groups is to convince the government actors (the veto players) to sign settlement agreements. The ability of Aboriginal groups to do so, however, is conditioned heavily by historical and cultural legacies. These legacies do not prevent Aboriginal agency from occurring. Rather, they set out the constraints under which Aboriginal agency can occur. The rest of this book applies this framework to identify a particular set of Aboriginal strategies that seem necessary for treaty settlements to occur. These strategies are: adopting goals that are compatible to those of the Crown; minimizing confrontational tactics; fostering Aboriginal group cohesion as it relates to the treaty process; and encouraging positive government perceptions of the Aboriginal group.

Case Selection and Methodology

Rather than being a normative critique[7] of the treaty process, which already exists and is well established in the Aboriginal politics literature, this book makes an original contribution by developing a social scientific explanation of treaty settlements versus non-settlements in Canada. To accomplish this goal, the book analyses four cases, two of which are in the Yukon Territory: the Kwanlin Dün First Nation (completed negotiations), located in and around the capital city of Whitehorse, and the Kaska Nations of Liard First Nation and Ross River Dena Council (incomplete negotiations), located in the southeastern part of the Territory. The other two cases are the Inuit in the northeastern part of Labrador (completed) and the Innu in the southeastern and central parts of Labrador (incomplete).

Using the comparative case study approach to look at both completed and uncompleted treaty negotiations strengthens the generalizability of the study's findings towards a broader set of cases. For instance, Hanson and Kopstein (2005) argue that comparative scholars studying *successful* political development have "tended to ignore cases of institutional and developmental *failure* that might have helped to pinpoint the relative causal importance of particular independent variables deemed important for explaining outcomes in more widely analyzed cases" (emphasis added) (Hanson and Kopstein, 2005: 91). Looking at both completed and incomplete negotiations provides us with greater leverage in identifying key explanatory variables for not only the cases at hand, but possibly a wider set of similar cases.

The Labrador cases are interesting for additional reasons. First, the academic literature has generally ignored the experiences of the Innu and the Inuit in Labrador in favour of other claims such as those of Nunavut, Nisga'a, James Bay, and Inuvialuit. This omission is surprising, since both claims have had an immense impact on the government and peoples of Newfoundland and Labrador. Second, the Inuit claim especially needs further study since it contains a number of provisions that differ from those of other final agreements. Third, the Labrador Inuit claim was among the last of the major Inuit claims in Canada to be completed and the first to be completed in the Atlantic provinces. As such, the Labrador Inuit Final Agreement may not only set the template for a future agreement with the Innu, but may also do so for other Aboriginal groups in the Atlantic provinces. Finally, both the Inuit and the Innu entered the modern treaty process at about the same time, were subject to the discovery of a rich nickel deposit in Voisey's Bay, used professional negotiators for most of their negotiations, and were subject to the same set of federal and provincial processes and actors during negotiations. Yet their outcomes differed. Why?

The Yukon claims are ripe for study for a number of reasons. In addition to the value of comparing negotiations in a province to those in a territory, the Yukon claims are interesting because, much like the Labrador claims, the Yukon claims are understudied in the literature. For instance, a number of scholars have looked at the 1993 Yukon Umbrella Final Agreement, a document that set out the terms by which each of the Yukon First Nations were supposed to negotiate their individual agreements. However, little, if any, attention has been paid to the actual individual agreements. The Kwanlin Dün claim, for instance, has been virtually ignored in the literature despite it being the first claim settled involving land located in a major Canadian city. The fact that Kwanlin Dün officials were able to sign a final agreement despite claiming land in the territorial capital is important for understanding how Aboriginal groups who have claimed municipal land in other major cities in Canada, such as Vancouver, can settle their claims.

The Kwanlin Dün First Nation's case is also worthy of study because this First Nation was able to complete a final agreement despite significant obstacles. Media reports and key informants indicated that the Kwanlin Dün was thought to be the most unlikely, or at least would be among the last, of the Yukon First Nations to get a deal done (see, for instance, Northern Native Broadcasting Yukon, 1997; Small, 2001b). It was given little prospect of success because the Kwanlin Dün membership is an amalgam of, on the one hand, "traditional" members from around Whitehorse and the Lake Laberge (north of Whitehorse) areas and of, on the other, Indians from other First Nations across the territory who had moved to Whitehorse (Koepke, 2006; Small, 2001a). Federal policy at the time required that these "come from aways" become band members of the Whitehorse Indian Band (the predecessor of the Kwanlin Dün First Nation) for the purposes of administering Indian Act programs and services. This mix of different Indian peoples created significant internal cohesion problems and intense political rivalries within the First Nation. The Kwanlin Dün negotiations were also complicated by the fact that, as mentioned above, the band was claiming large parts of the city of Whitehorse, including parts of the waterfront, which the City of Whitehorse was interested in developing. Negotiators, policy makers, and observers at the time doubted whether the Kwanlin Dün and the City of Whitehorse could reconcile their competing interests in municipal lands.

The Kaska have also been ignored in the literature, yet are also worthy of further study for two main reasons, in addition to the ones mentioned above. First, studying them is useful for understanding the effect of internal politics on land claims negotiations. In the eyes of the Crown, the Kaska are in fact five separate First Nations: two in the Yukon Territory – Liard First Nation near Watson Lake and Ross River Dena Council near Ross River – and three in northern British Columbia. In the minds of the Kaska, however, they constitute one Kaska Nation, politically represented by the Kaska Tribal Council. For much of their negotiating history, the Liard First Nation and the Ross River Dena Council have negotiated at separate tables towards separate agreements. However, beginning in the late 1980s and more prominently in the 1990s, they began to adopt a "one Kaska Nation" approach. As part of this approach, they demanded one set of negotiations and one deal for all the Kaska. At first, the governments refused their demands, but in the late 1990s they agreed to negotiate with the two Yukon First Nations at one table and with the three BC Kaska First Nations at another table.

Other groups have emulated this "one nation" approach. For instance, the Innu communities of Sheshatshiu and Natuashish in Labrador created Innu Nation to represent their interests at the negotiating table. Similarly, the Inuit communities in Labrador created the Labrador Inuit Association to negotiate their claim in 1977. Other Aboriginal groups have taken the opposite approach, separating into multiple groups for the purposes of negotiating their own individual land claims agreements. The Kwanlin Dün and the Ta'an Kwäch'än First Nations, for instance, were amalgamated into the Whitehorse Indian Band, until the federal government separated them in 1998 to negotiate their own final agreements.

Second, the Kaska are worthy of further study because they have long employed the same group of professional negotiators to negotiate their claim. Professional negotiators, some argue, are crucial for completing comprehensive land claims agreements in Canada (see for instance Penikett, 2006 [book]). Indeed, in the early summer of 2002, the Kaska negotiators had come to an agreement with their federal and territorial counterparts on a comprehensive land claims package, and the Kaska negotiators agreed to present the package to their peoples. To date, however, the federal and territorial governments have yet to receive a formal response from the Kaska. Nonetheless, federal and territorial officials acknowledge that the lack of a formal response indicates that the Kaska have rejected the package. This conclusion is confirmed through discussions with Kaska negotiators and begs the question: why have the Kaska failed to complete a treaty despite employing professional negotiators for many years?

To study the negotiating experiences of the Kwanlin Dün, the Kaska, the Inuit, and the Innu, in February 2006 I visited Happy Valley–Goose Bay, Sheshatshiu (Innu community), Natuashish (Innu community), Nain (Inuit community), Makkovik (Inuit community), and St John's in Newfoundland and Labrador. In October 2006, I visited Vancouver and Lower Post (Kaska), both in British Columbia, as well as Whitehorse (Kwanlin Dün), Ross River (Kaska), and Watson Lake (Kaska) in the Yukon Territory. I spent a total of five and a half weeks in these areas interviewing sixty-five government and Aboriginal participants. I also conducted five phone interviews with Aboriginal and government officials in British Columbia for the section on incremental treaty agreements in chapter 4. The interviewees themselves were Aboriginal, federal, and provincial/territorial politicians; senior or mid-level bureaucrats; legal counsel; and government and external negotiators. I also spoke with Aboriginal elders and citizens, City of Whitehorse politicians, and a number of informed observers who had been involved in either the negotiations themselves as participants, or in other First Nations' negotiations and were now living in the communities studied in this book. The interviews were semi-structured open, ranging anywhere from thirty minutes to two hours in length. Of the seventy individuals I interviewed, thirty were government officials and forty were Aboriginal officials. Throughout the text, I identify material and evidence gathered from these interviewees through the use of in-text citations, listing information about the interviewees in the bibliography unless the interviewees requested anonymity.

The Plan of the Book

This book is organized as follows. Chapter 1 sets the stage for the rest of the book by describing the institutional framework and the preferences and incentives of the negotiating actors. Chapter 2 presents the case studies of the Innu and the Inuit in Labrador, while chapter 3 describes and analyses the Yukon cases. From these chapters, I identify a set of strategies that seem to be crucial for producing settlements and non-settlements in Canada. I also note how the ability of Aboriginal groups to adopt these strategies is conditioned by their historical interactions with the Canadian state, aspects of their Indigenous cultures, and the actions of their leaders. Chapter 4 reflects on these findings and outlines a number of options available to Aboriginal groups that have yet to complete a treaty: keep negotiating; seek negotiation mechanisms within the process that may speed things up; or drop out of negotiations and pursue a number of alternatives that may help the Aboriginal group to increase its negotiating capacity, establish self-government, and acquire treaty-like benefits. A short conclusion reiterates the book's main findings and discusses its applicability to other cases and areas of study within the fields of Aboriginal politics and Canadian political science.

Chapter One

Setting the Stage: The Context of Modern Treaty Negotiations in Canada[1]

This chapter sets the stage for the rest of the book by first describing the institutional framework and players involved in the comprehensive land claims process and then specifying the preferences and incentives of the Aboriginal and non-Aboriginal actors. It finds that the institutional framework of the modern treaty process privileges the government actors over the Aboriginal ones. As a result, Aboriginal participants who want to complete treaties must somehow convince the Crown that a completed treaty is a preferable outcome. On the basis of these findings, subsequent chapters examine the experiences of four particular Aboriginal groups in order to identify the types of strategies that Aboriginal groups must use to convince the Crown to complete treaties, the conditioning influences that affect the ability of Aboriginal groups to choose these strategies, and the role that Aboriginal leaders play in mitigating these conditioning influences.

The Comprehensive Land Claims Process: The Rules and the Players

The federal government created the comprehensive land claims (CLC) process in 1973 to facilitate the exchange of undefined Aboriginal rights for a set of specific treaty rights. When the federal government created the process in 1973, it had no formal process to follow once an Aboriginal group submitted a claim. In 1981 the federal government adopted a formal process called "In All Fairness," to which it made major modifications in 1986 (Abele, 1986; Alcantara, 2009), followed by a number of relatively minor changes in the 1990s and 2000s.[2] Today, under the CLC process, an Aboriginal group submits a statement of intent to the federal and relevant sub-national governments to prove three things: that its rights to its claimed lands have never been extinguished; that it has historically occupied and used its claimed lands to the exclusion of other groups; and, finally, that it is a clearly identifiable and recognizable Aboriginal group (Indian and Northern Affairs Canada, 1998: 5; RCAP, 1996: 536–7). These requirements, which were established by the federal government with no input from Aboriginal stakeholders, have remained essentially unchanged over time.

Once these requirements are met, the three parties can begin negotiating a framework agreement. This agreement sets out the issues that are to be negotiated, how they will be negotiated, and by what date they must be resolved. A comprehensive land claims agreement can only address a limited range of issues, established by the Crown, and must in the end provide a full, certain, and final listing of all the rights and lands that a group may have now and in the future. The following excerpt from the federal policy guide lists some of the issues that are available for negotiations. Afterwards, I list the typical chapters in an agreement-in-principle.

> Under this approach, the range of matters that the federal government would see as subjects for negotiation could include all, some, or parts of the following: establishment of governing structures; internal constitutions; elections; leadership selection processes; membership; marriage; adoption and child welfare; Aboriginal language; culture and religion; education; health; social services; administration/enforcement of Aboriginal laws, including the establishment of Aboriginal courts or tribunals and the creation of offences of the type normally created by local or regional governments for contravention of their laws; policing; property rights, including succession and estates; land management, including: zoning; service fees; land tenure and access, and expropriation of Aboriginal land by Aboriginal governments for their own public purposes; natural resources management; agriculture; hunting, fishing and trapping on Aboriginal lands; taxation in respect of direct taxes and property taxes of members; transfer and management of monies and group assets; management of public works and infrastructure; housing; local transportation; licensing, regulation and operation of businesses located on Aboriginal lands. (Indian and Northern Affairs Canada, 1995)

In the following areas, Aboriginal groups may gain some power but federal and/or provincial law making authority is paramount: "divorce; labour/training; administration of justice issues, including matters related to the administration and enforcement of laws of other jurisdictions which might include certain criminal laws; penitentiaries and parole; environmental protection, assessment and pollution prevention; fisheries co-management; migratory birds co-management; gaming; emergency preparedness" (Indian and Northern Affairs Canada, 1995). Finally, the federal government retains law making authority over "(i) powers related to Canadian sovereignty, defence and external relations; and (ii) other national interest powers" (ibid.).

Once a framework agreement is achieved, the parties negotiate a non–legally binding agreement-in-principle (AIP). AIP negotiations are by far the most difficult and time consuming part of the process. As required by the Crown, most AIPs contain chapters on eligibility and enrolment in the Aboriginal group, land, access, economic development, culture and heritage, water management, fish and wildlife, migratory birds, forest resources, harvesting, environmental assessment, taxation, dispute resolution, implementation, compensation, and sometimes self-government. The AIP does not have to resolve all negotiation issues. Rather, it can leave some issues for final agreement negotiations. Typically, for instance, the negotiating parties wait until final agreement negotiations to select the actual parcels of settlement land to be included in the final agreement. The parties also tend to wait until this stage to negotiate the exact wording of the "cede, release, and surrender" provision, the clause that settles the nature and ownership of all lands subject to the treaty (Alcantara, 2009).

Although it is not legally binding, the AIP is usually used as the template for the final agreement. Previously, an AIP did not need to be ratified for final agreement negotiations to begin. However, this policy was changed after a number of Aboriginal communities failed to ratify their final agreements. To reduce the possibility that future final agreements will be rejected, federal policy now requires that all Aboriginal groups ratify their AIPs before final agreement negotiations can begin.

The purpose of the final agreement is to translate the AIP into a modern treaty, formalizing the negotiated terms. For instance, the final agreement sets out the settlement lands and land management powers that the Aboriginal group gains and clarifies the roles and responsibilities of each level of government in the settlement and non-settlement lands. Once signed, ratified, and enacted by laws passed in Parliament and the relevant sub-national legislature, the final agreement becomes a constitutional document under section 35 and guides future interactions and disputes between the signatories and the Aboriginal and non-Aboriginal peoples affected by the treaty.[3]

The negotiating parties in comprehensive land claims negotiations are the Aboriginal groups, the federal government, and the relevant provincial or territorial governments where the Aboriginal groups are located. For the federal side, the lead agency overseeing negotiations is Indian and Northern Affairs Canada (INAC) (Graham, 1987: 240). INAC undertakes negotiations according to guidelines set out in the federal comprehensive land claims policy and, more importantly, according to the negotiation mandates given to it by the federal cabinet. These mandates set out the scope and range of the lands, powers, and jurisdictions that the federal negotiating team can negotiate (Penikett, 2006 [book]: 161–73; Dewar, 2009: 75).

Compared to other government actors, INAC's position as the lead agency in negotiations gives it substantial power over negotiations (Serson, 2006). The most influential INAC officials are the chief federal negotiators and the minister and deputy minister. The chief federal negotiators, who are external consultants hired on contract, act as the federal government's main liaison with the negotiating Aboriginal groups, whereas the minister and deputy minister have the task of *informing* and, most importantly, *seeking agreement* from fellow ministers and deputy ministers in such departments as Finance, Industry, Justice, Environment, and Fisheries and Oceans regarding the land claims provisions that may affect their ministries. In many instances, opposition to negotiated positions tends to come from ministers and deputy ministers in other departments who tend to have a veto on issues that affect their departments and are more reluctant to cede ground on issues like taxation, environmental protection, and fish and wildlife management (Dewar, 2009: 75). INAC ministers and deputy ministers, therefore, become important "middlemen" for building bridges between the positions being negotiated at the treaty table and the positions held by ministers and deputy ministers in other government departments.

INAC officials also have significant influence on negotiation mandates. Although cabinet has the final say over negotiation mandates, it usually calls upon INAC officials to draft the initial mandates for cabinet consideration. Once these are approved, INAC's minister and deputy minister enforce the mandates and are responsible for seeking modifications to them on behalf of Aboriginal groups and the territorial/provincial governments. Moreover, the INAC's minister and deputy minister are the key officials who ensure that different government departments adhere to the mandates drafted by cabinet.

Other federal officials who can have a substantial influence on land claims negotiations are the prime minister and key figures in such central agencies as the Privy Council Office, the Prime Minister's Office, and Finance; their influence stems from the fact that Canada's parliamentary system is executive-dominated (Bakvis, 2001; Savoie, 1999; Thomas, 1999). A motivated prime minister, for instance, can unilaterally alter a mandate to speed up or delay the process, regardless of cabinet objections (see Dewar, 2009: 78). Nonetheless, INAC remains the most important federal agency in influencing comprehensive land claims negotiations because of its position as the lead agency in conducting negotiations with the Aboriginal groups, and in moving land claims provisions through the machinery of the federal government (Graham, 1987: 240; Serson, 2006; but also see Abele and Graham, 1988: 123 and Dewar, 2009: 75–6).

At the provincial level, historically speaking, many provinces did not have a ministry solely dedicated to Aboriginal affairs. Usually, this ministry or secretariat, if it existed, was tied to another line department or was situated within the office of the premier. In Newfoundland and Labrador, for example, the Aboriginal affairs portfolio is located in the Department of Labrador and Aboriginal Affairs. Under previous administrations, such as that of Premier Clyde Wells (1989–96), the minister responsible for Aboriginal Affairs was the premier himself (Haysom, 1990). As at the federal level, the provincial Aboriginal Affairs department is the lead agency in land claims negotiations. It helps cabinet draft negotiation mandates, enforces them, and makes recommendations on altering them. It takes the lead in coordinating and undertaking the negotiations themselves, and plays an important role in acting as a liaison with other departments and the premier. In general, as at the federal level, provincial Aboriginal Affairs departments have substantial control over how negotiations unfold, subject to the influence of the premier.

In contrast to territorial land claims negotiations, provinces have constitutional ownership and jurisdiction over many of the important negotiation stakes.[4] Their jurisdiction includes ownership of lands and natural resources, municipalities, taxation, land use planning, water management, self-government powers such as education and the administration of justice, and fish and wildlife. The federal government recognizes the importance of provincial governments in land claims negotiations; indeed, federal policy declares that provincial governments must be involved in Aboriginal land claims located within provincial boundaries.[5] As a result, a large chunk of the actual negotiating tends to occur between the provincial government and the Aboriginal groups. The fact that provincial governments do a lot of the negotiating is important because, as Christa Scholtz (2006) has found, sub-national (provincial) governments tend to be more reluctant than national ones to adopt Aboriginal treaty negotiation policies. By extension, they tend to be more reluctant to complete modern treaties because treaties tend to have a larger effect on provincial lands, powers, and jurisdictions.

Until the late 1980s, territorial governments tended to have a smaller role in comprehensive land claims negotiations because they were creatures of the federal government and only had jurisdiction over their lands at the pleasure of the federal government (Coates and Powell, 1989: 112). However, as a result of devolution, over time the Canadian territories have developed into pseudo-provinces, with powers and responsibilities that mimic provincial ones (Cameron and White, 1995; Small, 2002a; White, 2002b: 17). Although comprehensive land claims negotiations in the territories were originally bilateral, they are now trilateral, with the territorial government acting as the key negotiating government. A number of Yukon government officials and others told me that territorial governments are the primary government negotiators in the final stages of negotiations because it is their governments and their citizens who will have to live with the aftermath of a final agreement (Armour, 2006; Beaudoin, 2006; Flynn, 2006; McCullough, 2006; Dave Porter, 2006; see also Small, 2002d). In the Yukon Territory, this was true to the extent that most of the final negotiations revolved around issues like land selection and jurisdiction, most of which were of more concern to the territorial government than the federal government. Officials involved with the Labrador negotiations mentioned the same thing, noting that provincial negotiators were more likely to be the dominant negotiators than the federal government.[6]

At the territorial level, the land claims secretariat or the Aboriginal Affairs ministry is in charge of supervising and conducting comprehensive land claims negotiations. In the Yukon Territory, the land claims secretariat belongs to the office of the premier. This institutional setting has powerful implications for the political clout of the secretariat, especially since the Yukon Territory employs a parliamentary system with political parties and a vigorous form of responsible government

(McCormick, 2001).[7] As a result, Yukon land claims officials benefit from having the premier as their minister because it makes it easier to establish and modify negotiation mandates, seek agreement and advice from other departments, and receive political direction, depending on the premier's interest (Armour, 2006; Flynn, 2006; McCullough, 2006).

The final negotiating party in comprehensive land claims negotiations is the Aboriginal group. Usually, it is represented by negotiators hired by either the band council or some sort of umbrella organization formed to represent an Aboriginal community or communities in negotiations. For instance, in Labrador, the Inuit communities of Nain, Rigolet, Hopedale, Postville, Makkovik, and the Upper Lake Melville area near Happy Valley–Goose Bay, were represented by an elected Labrador Inuit Association (LIA) at the negotiating table. The Labrador Innu formed Innu Nation to represent their two communities (Sheshatshiu and Natuashish) during their land claims negotiations.

In the Yukon, all fourteen First Nations joined together to form the Council for Yukon Indians to negotiate an Umbrella Final Agreement. The Umbrella agreement was meant to provide a common basis from which each individual First Nation would negotiate an individual final agreement. For instance, after the Umbrella Final Agreement was completed in 1993, the Kwanlin Dün First Nation began negotiations in the late 1990s and completed its final agreement in 2005. The two Kaska Nations of Ross River and Liard First Nation, by contrast, chose to form an umbrella organization called the Kaska Tribal Council to represent their interests during Umbrella and final agreement negotiations for their individual communities. Their decision to create the Kaska Tribal Council was the result of a growing pan-Kaska nationalism movement. Today, the Kaska Tribal Council represents the Ross River Dena Council and Liard First Nation in the Yukon Territory and the three Kaska First Nations in British Columbia. The Kaska maintain that both the BC provincial government and the Yukon territorial government must negotiate a comprehensive land claims agreement with the Kaska Tribal Council rather than with the individual Kaska First Nations.

Preferences and Incentives

Having described the basic rules and players involved in modern treaty negotiations, I will now draw upon a variety of data to accomplish a number of things. First, following the theoretical assumptions specified in the introductory chapter, I will describe the primary motivations that drive government and Aboriginal actors in the modern treaty process to show how differences in negotiating preferences may help explain settlements and non-settlements in Canada. Second, I will specify the incentive structures influencing the negotiating actors to suggest that government actors face strong disincentives to complete treaties, while Aboriginal actors face strong incentives to complete treaties. Third, and relatedly, I will describe how Aboriginal groups in the modern treaty process are in a relatively weaker bargaining position than Crown actors, meaning that in light of divergent preferences and incentives, Aboriginal groups will have to find the right strategies to convince government actors to complete treaties. Finally, and throughout the rest of this chapter, I will illustrate that at the aggregate level, federal, provincial, and Aboriginal actors can be treated as unitary actors, at least in the context of comprehensive land claims negotiations. There are some exceptions that matter, and these are addressed later on in the book in the sections on factors that affect the speed of negotiations and on Aboriginal leadership, but it is empirically accurate and theoretically useful to treat negotiating actors at the aggregate level as unitary when specifying the preferences and incentives of federal, provincial, and Aboriginal governments.[8] In short, the following section gives empirical life to the theoretical assumptions specified in the introductory chapter.

Preferences

The federal government in comprehensive land claims negotiations is primarily interested in ensuring certainty and finality for the purposes of encouraging economic development (Mitchell, 1996: 343–4, 347; Rynard, 2000: 232).[9] It is also interested in empowering Aboriginal peoples by helping them to increase their capacity for governance and self-sufficiency (Serson, 2006; Shafto, 2006). According to INAC's (1998) *Federal Policy for the Settlement of Native Claims*:

> The primary purpose of comprehensive claims settlements is to conclude agreements with Aboriginal groups that will resolve the debates and legal ambiguities associated with the common law concept of Aboriginal rights and title. Uncertainty with respect to the legal status of lands and resources, which has been created by a lack of political agreement with Aboriginal groups, is a barrier to economic development for all Canadians and has hindered the full participation of Aboriginal peoples in land and resource management. (5)

These policy goals have been confirmed by Aboriginal, federal, provincial, and territorial interviewees, who state that the federal government's main goal is to foster and encourage economic development, usually to reap the revenues generated from them (Andersen III, 2006; Andrew, 2006; John-Pierre Ashini, 2006; Gingell, 2006; Innes, 2006; Mitander, 2006; Serson, 2006; Shafto, 2006). Government actions to facilitate economic development, however, have not always respected Aboriginal concerns or interests. In many instances and despite opposition from Aboriginal groups, the federal government has provided permits, generous tax write-offs, and infrastructure to encourage businesses to engage in economic development on Aboriginal lands (Angus, 1992: 68–9; McPherson, 2003: 142; Miller, 2000: 365–6; Nuke, 2006).

The goals of the Newfoundland and Labrador government are similar to those of the federal government. Although the provincial government does not have a formal land claims policy akin to the federal one, it has clearly shown an overwhelming interest in economic development, especially since the collapse of the fishing industry (Dyck, 1996: 31; Summers, 2001: 23). In light of this collapse and the historical difficulties that it has had in generating wealth, provincial government officials see land claims agreements as important mechanisms for generating much-needed economic development opportunities. According to Minister Ernest McLean (2001), "Successful land claims negotiations with the LIA and the Innu will ensure economic, legal and social certainty for governance and business and social development." Settling these claims is necessary because Labrador is the key to the economic health of the entire province. According to Minister Tom Rideout (2004),

> The goal of this government is to achieve economic health for the province. Building the economic health of Labrador is a key part of that plan. We are building a strong foundation that will enable all regions of the province to achieve their enormous potential. From what I have seen during my visit to Labrador, the potential there is certainly enormous ... As we move forward with implementing the strategy, our investments will be made where they will have the most positive impact for all regions of the province.

Others have reiterated that economic development should benefit all provincial citizens and should not be carried out at the expense of Aboriginal peoples in the province (Pelley, 2006). "It is imperative that we ensure any land claim settlement reached with the Inuit and Innu are [*sic*] fair to all Labradorians – Aboriginal and non-Aboriginal" (Lush, 2001). In sum,

> The provincial government's objective in negotiating comprehensive land claim agreements is to achieve certain and final settlement of Aboriginal claims to the territory within the Province. Certainty as to the ownership of lands and how such lands are to be managed will provide a more stable environment for development and investment ... Settlement of the land claim is necessary to provide for the long term economic and social development of the province, and contribute to the economic, social and cultural development of Labrador Inuit claimants. Negotiations are intended to accommodate the interests of Labrador Inuit, governments and third parties. (Executive Council, 1997)

The actions of the provincial government, however, have not always reflected the belief that economic development should benefit both Aboriginal and non-Aboriginal peoples. Between the 1970s and 1990s, the provincial government engaged in a number of economic development projects in Labrador without consulting the Innu or the Inuit. These projects included commercial logging, hydroelectric development, fishing, and mining (Tony Andersen, 2006; Nuke, 2006; Rich, 2006).[10] According to members of both Aboriginal groups, the proportion of revenues that governments and businesses have derived from these projects dwarfs the amount that the Aboriginal groups have received (Tony Andersen, 2006; Andrew, 2006; John-Pierre Ashini, 2006; Jararuse, 2006; Nuke, 2006; Riche, 2006).

Much like the Newfoundland and Labrador government, the Yukon territorial government is focused on maximizing the development of its lands for the purposes of enhancing the well-being of its citizens (Cameron and White, 1995: 12; Flynn, 2006; McArthur, 2006; McCullough, 2006; McCormick, 2001: 369; Penikett, 2006 [book]; Waddell, 2001). For instance, the Yukon government has long lobbied the federal government to devolve control over Yukon lands and resources to the territorial government (Armour, 2006; McArthur, 2006; McCormick, 2001; McCullough, 2006; Penikett, 2006 [interview]). Successive Yukon governments felt that the territory's lands and resources could only be properly developed by eliminating federal jurisdiction, which it finally accomplished in 2003 with the negotiation of the Yukon Devolution Transfer Agreement. Land and resource issues have also driven land claims negotiations. The Yukon government was strongly interested in establishing certainty in areas that were ripe for development but where title was potentially unclear and not subject to third-party interests. As in the Labrador case, the Yukon territorial government, the federal government, and the resource industry engaged in economic development on Yukon Aboriginal lands before and during negotiations. According to Aboriginal and Yukon government officials, there was never a time during negotiations when economic development was frozen except for those lands that the federal, territorial, and Aboriginal representatives agreed to freeze.[11]

Aboriginal interests, in contrast, are much broader. In general, Aboriginal peoples want to maximize their control over their traditional lands to protect their traditional ways of life and practices, derive revenues and jobs from economic development, and take control of their lives in areas such as education, health, law enforcement, environmental protection, culture, heritage, fishing, and hunting (Andrew, 2006; Beaudoin, 2006; Brown, 2006; Jack, 1990: 23; Joe, 2006; Mitander, 2006; Nuke, 2006; O'Brien, 2006; Dave Porter, 2006; Samson et al., 1999: 30–4; Wadden, 1991: 200).

There are some differences among the four Aboriginal groups studied in this book. The most important difference is the way in which each group views its position relative to Canada, with some groups like the Innu being driven more by ideology and others, like the Inuit, being driven more by pragmatism. The Innu leaders, negotiators, and community members originally came to the table with the notion that any agreement had to recognize Innu sovereignty (Andrew, 2006; Innes, 2006; Innu Nation, 1995: 175; Pelley, 2006; Wadden, 1991: 200). Their desire for sovereignty, which is tied to their relationship to the land, has softened over time, but some Innu leaders continue to hold Innu sovereignty as the end goal for their comprehensive land claims agreement. The same is generally true for the Kaska nations. Kaska leaders and community members were originally opposed and continued to be opposed to any sort of "cede, release, and surrender" of their traditional lands. They believe very much in the idea that any final agreement must confirm, not extinguish, their Aboriginal title. For instance, a 2003 bilateral agreement signed between the Kaska and the Yukon territorial government affirms that the "Yukon [government] acknowledged, in agreements entered into with the Kaska in January 1997, that the Kaska have Aboriginal rights, titles and interest in and to the Kaska Traditional Territory in the Yukon" (preamble). In practice, section 3 of the bilateral agreement requires Kaska consent before any proposed economic development projects on Kaska land can occur. The key point here is that most Kaska leaders, elders, and community members reject "cede, release, and surrender." Rather, they desire a guarantee of their Aboriginal title to *all* of their traditional territories (Armour, 2006; Hanson, 2006; McCullough, 2006; Dave Porter, 2006; Van Bibber, 2006; Walsh, 2006).

Contrast this to Inuit leaders and negotiators, who have rarely, if ever, invoked the language of sovereignty. They have always preferred to negotiate an agreement that safeguards their traditional ways of life and interests in economic development, and that allows them to take control over important policy areas through some form of self-government *within* the federation. Indeed, the language and strategies used by Inuit leaders (LIA presidents, vice-presidents, board members, negotiators, and elders) were consistently based on conciliation, compromise, and accommodation (Tony Andersen, 2006; Barbour, 2006; Haysom, 2006; Hibbs, 2006; Pain, 2006; Rowell, 2006; see also McPherson, 2003: 129 regarding the Inuit's general propensity for consensus building rather than confrontation). For instance, Labrador Inuit Association chief negotiator Toby Andersen (2001) has said: "We hope there will be benefits in the land claims settlement for non-Aboriginal as well as for Aboriginal peoples." Former LIA president and former Nunatsiavut president William Andersen III (1990: 20) has said, "With respect to land claims, we've chosen a route of negotiation rather than confrontation. And we are not opposed to development, provided environmental standards are met. But the people in the area should have first priority. It makes no difference to us who benefits from development as long as it's the people of Labrador."

The views of Kwanlin Dün leaders and negotiators on sovereignty and negotiations are similar to those of Inuit officials. Since the beginning of the twentieth century, the Kwanlin Dün First Nation has been one of the strongest proponents among the Yukon First Nations for a treaty settlement. Many of the leaders who drove the original claim, the agreement-in-principle negotiations, and the Umbrella Final Agreement (UFA) negotiations were from the Kwanlin Dün First Nation. Chief Bose, for instance, asked Ottawa in the early 1900s to negotiate a land claim, only to be refused (Joe, 2006; Mitander, 2006). Chief Elijah Smith in the early 1970s was instrumental in writing and presenting the Yukon First Nations statement of claim, *Together Today for Our Children Tomorrow*, to the federal government in 1973 (Coates, 1991: 237–8; Yukon Native Brotherhood, 1973). Kwanlin Dün Chief Rick O'Brien (who later became an important leader within the Council for Yukon First Nations) was instrumental in the late 1990s and early 2000s in building a new Kwanlin Dün land claims department with a mandate to complete negotiations after the previous department fell apart due to political infighting. Chief Mike Smith was a chief of the Council for Yukon First Nations in the mid-1980s, a Kwanlin Dün land claims negotiator and lawyer in the late 1990s and early 2000s, and chief of Kwanlin Dün First Nation from 2003 onwards. All these leaders were interested in negotiations and were willing to engage in them without insisting on Aboriginal sovereignty. In addition to leadership effects, further evidence of the Kwanlin Dün's preference to "avoid" the language of sovereignty during negotiations comes from the fact that it adopted the Umbrella Final Agreement as its final agreement with some minor modifications as permitted by the UFA. More importantly, Kwanlin Dün's final agreement contains the "cede, release, and surrender" provision (Kwanlin Dün Final Agreement, 2005).

Differing Incentives to Negotiate and to Delay[12]

Federal, provincial, and territorial politicians, bureaucrats, and negotiators have powerful incentives as well as resources to delay completing an agreement. The actual CLC process, with its formal rules and procedures, places Aboriginal groups in a weaker position relative to federal, provincial, and territorial governments. The negotiating process forces Aboriginal groups to prove to the governments that their claims are valid and therefore acceptable for negotiations. Aboriginal groups must adopt Western standards of knowledge, proof, discourse, and negotiation processes if they want negotiations to proceed. Rather than being able to use their traditional knowledge, languages, and oral histories in negotiations, they are forced to produce maps, hire Euro-Canadian anthropologists, linguists, lawyers, and historians to prepare and document their claims, and engage in formal proposal/counter-proposal negotiations, all in the English language (Ben Andrew, 2006; John-Pierre Ashini, 2006; Macklem, 2001: 271–2; McPherson, 2003: 140; Michel, 2006; Samson, 2003). This last requirement can be a significant problem for Aboriginal groups like the Innu and the Kaska, among the majority of whose members traditional languages remain strong. Aboriginal groups also have little power to influence the agenda as they can only negotiate those responsibilities and jurisdictions that are listed under the federal comprehensive land claims policy (INAC, 1998: 7–8).

Moreover, the government can at any time declare that certain lands are no longer up for discussion. For example, in 1994, the Voisey's Bay area of Labrador was taken off the table after large nickel deposits were found there.

In essence, under the CLC process, the federal, provincial, and territorial governments have become rights-granting entities while Aboriginal groups have become petitioners, forced to prove the validity of their claims to the governments before they can ask the governments to cede to them land, rights, self-government, and jurisdiction (Ben Andrew, 2006; Backhouse and McRae, 2002: 58; Samson, 2003). This rights-granting status is enhanced by the sovereign power that the governments enjoy under the Constitution Act of 1982 (see Macklem, 2001: 87). The constitution, which is an important aspect of the institutional context, gives the federal government, the Newfoundland and Labrador government, and the Yukon territorial government a wide range of powers over the land, water, and peoples of Canada. These governments have frequently exercised their powers without consulting the Aboriginal peoples in those areas (Andersen III, 2006; Tony Andersen, 2006; Ben Andrew, 2006; Napes Ashini, 1992: 124; Marshall, 2006; Nui, 2006; Rich, 2006). For instance, according to Wadden (1991: 45), "Canadian governments have always acted as though the Innu, and their land rights in Nitassinan,[13] do not exist. Mines, hydroelectric projects and pulp and paper mills have sprouted up all over the Innu homeland during this century, enriching the coffers of provincial governments and multinational companies but wrecking [sic] havoc with Innu lives." Peter Penashue, former Innu Nation president, expresses his people's exasperation with the federal and provincial governments' unilateral actions on Innu land. "When we tried to express ourselves, they put us in jail in St John's and Stephenville. We are vulnerable and easy to put in jail. We don't have a military. We don't have voting power; we are small in numbers" (Penashue, 1992: 129).[14]

The other three Aboriginal groups examined in this book have also experienced unilateral action on their claimed lands. For instance, the Inuit have had to deal with the federal and provincial governments imposing fishing and environmental regulations on them, harvesting their fish, wildlife, and forests, and developing Voisey's Bay, all without Inuit consent or consultation (Tony Andersen, 2006; Andersen III, 2006; Barbour, 2006). The Kwanlin Dün has had to deal with "illegal" economic development on its traditional lands located in the city of Whitehorse. The Kaska nations have long had to deal with "illegal" resource development in the form of mines and lumber harvesting on their traditional lands. In the 1960s, the governments and industry cooperated to open a mine on Kaska lands in Faro without obtaining Kaska consent (Dave Porter, 2006; Sterriah, 2006; Sharp, 1976). In short, the power relations (as a result of the distribution of political resources and the institutional context) clearly favour the federal, provincial, and territorial governments.

Government incentives to drag out negotiations are also affected by the negotiation stakes. Many of the jurisdictional powers and lands involved in comprehensive land claims negotiations belong to the provinces or greatly affect the territories. In Newfoundland and Labrador, the federal government has an interest in cash transfers, taxation, implementation costs, fisheries, migratory birds, and environmental protection. The province, by contrast, has jurisdiction over inland water, economic development, renewable and non-renewable resources, lands, environmental protection, and local governance. Overall, the provincial government has much more at stake in negotiations than the federal government (Carter, 2006; Feit, 1980; Pelley, 2006). This jurisdictional situation means that the main task of Aboriginal groups is to convince the province that a modern treaty is consistent with its interests (Hawco, 2006; INAC, 1998: 6–7; Rowell, 2006).

In the Yukon Territory, the federal government had jurisdiction over Yukon lands and resources for the majority of the land claims negotiations. However, these issues were more important to the Yukon territorial government (YTG) because once CLC negotiations were completed, the federal government would withdraw from the Yukon, leaving the YTG to deal with the Aboriginal and non-Aboriginal peoples affected by the treaties. Moreover, the territorial government had more at stake because it knew that the land claims agreements would have a powerful effect on future land use and economic development in the territory. In the long run, the territorial government hoped to achieve quasi-provincial or provincial status and thus it had significant interest in ensuring that the treaties did not hinder its future ability to manage its lands and resources (Armour, 2006; McArthur, 2006; McCullough, 2006).

Mixed incentives to negotiate have come from Canadian courts. In *Delgamuukw v. British Columbia* (1997), the Supreme Court ruled that constitutionally protected Aboriginal rights can be infringed for the greater good of economic development. However, the ability to engage in economic development is not unfettered, since the Crown is still bound by its fiduciary duty to Aboriginal peoples to negotiate in good faith (Macklem, 2001: 252–3). Canadian courts have also ruled that provincial and territorial governments have a duty to consult about or accommodate Aboriginal interests (Penikett, 2006 [book]; RCAP, 1996).[15] Overall, according to Monture-Angus (1999), Canadian courts have generated mixed results in terms of advancing Aboriginal self-determination and independence in Canada.[16]

Other incentives to negotiate through to a treaty come from a growing awareness of Aboriginal rights. Former Deputy Minister of INAC Scott Serson (2006) has observed that bureaucrats and negotiators felt pressure to get a deal done after the publication of the Royal Commission on Aboriginal Peoples (RCAP 1996) and the federal government's response, *Gathering Strength*.[17] Federal bureaucrats felt they had to demonstrate that *Gathering Strength* could successfully accommodate the concerns raised in RCAP about treaty making in Canada. YTG officials have mentioned that in addition to the quest for legal certainty, they were also driven by a moral responsibility to correct the historical wrongs inflicted by the Crown on Yukon First Nations (Armour, 2006; Flynn, 2006; McCullough, 2006). Floyd McCormick (1997), however, has shown that, in general, government motivations stemming from rights are usually trumped by economic concerns. Economic concerns create disincentives to negotiate only when governments can engage in economic development on Aboriginal lands without having to negotiate a treaty. As long as government actors can engage in development without a treaty, they will be reluctant to negotiate simply because most of the time they can reap the rewards of development without a treaty. Recent litigation, however, has changed this situation somewhat.[18] Governments are now less likely and less able to engage in unilateral development on Aboriginal lands. Therefore, this disincentive, while still in effect, has been much less influential on government incentive structures from 2004 onwards.

In short, government incentives to negotiate come from judicial decisions and a growing awareness of rights, while stronger disincentives come from institutional structures like the constitutional division of powers and the nature of the federal comprehensive land claims process. The result is that government actors are willing to negotiate with Aboriginal groups but only at a slow pace; structural and economic imperatives seem to trump the influence of rights, making governments reluctant to negotiate.[19] It is clear that governments are interested in clearing the path for development. However, if governments can get away with developing lands without completing treaties, they will do so. For instance, the provincial government of British Columbia had been issuing permits to companies to develop Carrier Sekani First Nations lands despite the fact that it was negotiating with Carrier Sekani under the British Columbia Treaty Commission process. This situation prompted the Carrier Sekani First Nations to drop out of the BCTC process to pursue alternative mechanisms for controlling development on their lands (Brethour, 2007: A2).

Aboriginal groups, by contrast, have powerful incentives to negotiate final agreements. First and most important, they have no better options by which to satisfy their preferences within the current institutional framework. Members from all four Aboriginal groups in this study have mentioned that the comprehensive land claims process is the "only game in town" for achieving the type of control they want over their lands (Andersen III, 2006; Beaudoin, 2006; Dick, 2006; Hibbs, 2006; Jararuse, 2006; Dave Porter, 2006; Paul Rich, 2006; Riche, 2006; Sterriah, 2006). Aboriginal groups throughout Canada have considered and used litigation, but judicial outcomes are unpredictable and can be as damaging as helpful (Curry, 2007: A7; Diamond, 1985: 279; Feit, 1980: 163; Macklem and Townshend, 1992: 78–9; Monture-Angus, 1999; Penikett, 2006 [book]; Warren, 2006). This unpredictability, however, has not stopped the Kaska from being the most litigious First Nation in the Yukon Territory (Armour, 2006; Hanson, 2006; Koepke, 2006; Walsh, 2006). Nonetheless, there are a few Kaska negotiators who want to get back to the negotiating table, albeit on different terms than those of the UFA (Dave Porter, 2006; Sterriah, 2006; Walsh, 2006).

Some Aboriginal groups have used protest tactics, but these actions rarely lead to Aboriginal groups gaining the type of control they want. The Innu, in the 1980s and early 1990s, were one of the most active groups in Canada in their use of protests and other confrontational strategies (Alcantara, 2010). However, these strategies tended to generate unsatisfactory outcomes, and as a result the Innu have focused solely on negotiating since 2001 (Benuen, 2006; Innes, 2006; Riche, 2006; Rich, 2006).

Aboriginal groups face another incentive to negotiate, mainly that "once it became clear that development was going to happen even in the absence of a settlement, pressure began to grow at the community level to resolve claims and to 'catch a ride' on the development that was occurring" (Angus, 1992: 71). Aboriginal groups realize that governments will engage in economic development anyway, so coming to an agreement is necessary if they are to have a voice in how governments and businesses undertake those developments (Dick, 2006; Jararuse, 2006; Joe, 2006; Mitander, 2006; Dave Porter, 2006; Paul Rich, 2006; see also McPherson, 2003 regarding Inuit in Nunavut; and Rynard, 2001: 12–13 regarding the Cree in Quebec).

Conclusion

In summary, the institutional framework governing comprehensive land claims negotiations in Canada gives the federal, provincial, and territorial governments a significant advantage over participating Aboriginal groups. Although all the negotiating parties are influenced by incentive structures that pressure them to negotiate, the federal, provincial, and territorial governments are also subject to much stronger incentives to delay negotiations as much as possible. These incentives to delay are artefacts of the institutional structures that have arisen through the comprehensive land claims process.

Aboriginal groups begin the process by filing a statement of intent signalling their intention to negotiate a claim with the federal and relevant sub-national governments. Governments can respond in two ways. They can either refuse to accept the statement of intent because it fails to satisfy the requirements set out in government policy, or they can recognize the claim and begin negotiations. A claim is acceptable when an Aboriginal group can prove three things: that its rights to its claimed lands have never been extinguished; that it has historically occupied and used its claimed lands to the exclusion of other groups; and, finally, that it is a clearly identifiable and recognizable Aboriginal group (Indian and Northern Affairs Canada, 1998: 5; RCAP, 1996: 536–7). The acceptance by both levels of government is required for a claim to move forward. If a government refuses a land claim, then the Aboriginal group must prepare a new claim and file it with the governments. In the case of the Labrador Innu, it took fourteen years before it was able to submit a statement of claim that was acceptable to the federal and provincial governments. If the governments accept the claim, then the default negotiations path is prolonged negotiations because of the incentive structures that influence governments. On this path, negotiations take a very long time to complete. Although framework agreements tend to be signed relatively quickly, agreements-in-principle tend to take much longer to complete. For example, the Labrador Inuit completed a framework agreement in fourteen months and an agreement-in-principle in eleven years. Usually, it is in the agreement-in-principle negotiations stage when most negotiations stall, get suspended, or end.

Aboriginal groups can accelerate negotiations, but these efforts do not always lead to completed settlements. Rather, they can instead lead to alternatives to a completed treaty, such as an interim agreement or an incremental treaty agreement (described in greater detail in chapter 4), both of which may or may not lead to a final agreement. In the case of the Labrador Innu, accelerated negotiations led to a set of interim agreements on Voisey's Bay that ended up slowing negotiations down. Negotiations slowed because the interim agreements helped the government actors to achieve their preference for economic development without drastically altering the institutional framework, which is what a final agreement does. Contrast this situation to that of the Inuit, who despite signing interim agreements, were able to complete a final agreement. What explains this variation? The next two chapters attempt to answer this question more precisely by examining the experiences of four Aboriginal groups in Canada.

Chapter Two

The Innu and the Inuit in Labrador

In the mid- to late 1970s, both the Innu and the Inuit in Labrador submitted statements of intent to begin negotiating comprehensive land claims agreements with the Canadian Crown. As part of their original submissions, both groups claimed the Voisey's Bay area, which in 1994 was found to contain a multi-billion-dollar nickel deposit. Some commentators at the time believed that this discovery, combined with the provincial government's strong interest in mining-based economic development in Labrador, would allow the Inuit and the Innu to complete land claims settlements. Indeed, these were the lessons gleaned from the negotiations in Quebec by the James Bay Cree, who had supposedly completed a modern treaty in 1975 due to the Quebec government's strong interest in developing a massive hydro-electric project in northern Quebec. Up until the mid-1990s, progress on the Innu and the Inuit land claims agreements was minimal and slow-moving. The discovery of nickel in Voisey's Bay, however, accelerated both sets of negotiations, but only the Inuit completed a treaty, doing so in 2005. This chapter offers some reasons for why the Innu and the Inuit experienced different outcomes despite both being affected by the discovery of a major mineral deposit.

We begin with a short history and description of the two Aboriginal groups in Labrador that are the focus of this chapter. Next, we sketch out their individual comprehensive land claims negotiation histories before ending with an analysis of the factors that contributed to their divergent experiences. In short, the Labrador cases show that due to differing preferences, power structures, and incentives for negotiating, the role of the Aboriginal groups themselves is critical for explaining settlements and non-settlements in Canada.

Who Are the Inuit and the Innu?

Maps

Three maps are presented here. Map 2.1 illustrates the main cities, highways, and waterways of Labrador. Map 2.2 shows the lands over which the Labrador Inuit gained control through their land claims agreement. Map 2.3 shows Nitassinan, the traditional lands of the Innu.

A Brief History of the Inuit

The traditional territories of the Labrador Inuit are found in along the coast of the northeastern part of Labrador (Crowe, 1991: 17–18). Historically, most Inuit "lived in extended family units, place-groups or bands," related by blood with a common interest in specific hunting or resource areas (Nunatsiavut Government, 2006a). The Inuit were constantly on the move throughout the year, hunting for caribou, porcupine, and other game during the warmer months, and for seals and whales during the winter (Dorais, 2002: 135, 137–9).

First contact with Europeans occurred in the mid-sixteenth century when Basque whalers began to establish land stations on the southern parts of the northern mainland (Nunatsiavut Government, 2006a; Dorais, 2002: 133; McMillan and Yellowhorn, 2004: 288). By the 1620s, the Basque whalers had moved on to fishing areas near Greenland and were quickly replaced in the area by French and English whalers and fishermen. Increased contact would eventually lead to increased trade between Dutch, Basque, and French whalers and the Inuit (Dorais, 2002: 133). Eventually European traders established temporary trading posts in Inuit lands to facilitate the transfer of European goods to the Inuit along the northern coast.

In the late 1760s, Moravian missionaries, a protestant group based in Germany, applied for and received from the British Crown large tracts of land to establish trading posts and churches in Labrador. In 1771, the Moravians built a mission and a trading post in Nain to become the first Europeans to establish a permanent presence in the area. In 1790 they built schools in the areas of Nain, Okak, and Hopedale (Dorais, 2002: 133, 143; McMillan and Yellowhorn, 2004: 288; Nunatsiavut Government, 2006d). These Moravian communities would later evolve into the Inuit communities of Nain, Okak, Hopedale, and Hebron (Nunatsiavut Government, 2006d).

Map 2.1

The Moravians had an immense impact on Inuit society, culture, and life, all of which would have a mostly positive effect on the ability of the Inuit to complete a modern treaty. As the Inuit became more exposed to the Moravians, their life changed dramatically. Moravian trading posts in Inuit communities provided the Inuit with immediate access to European goods and expertise, so they became less dependent on travel during the winter and more willing to stay in the Moravian communities. Also contributing to a more sedentary life was the influence of the Moravian religion. Most of the Inuit eventually converted to Christianity and abandoned their nomadic, season-centred living habits to settle in the permanent Moravian mission-centred communities (Dorais, 2002: 142; Nunatsiavut Government, 2006d). By the end

Map 2.2

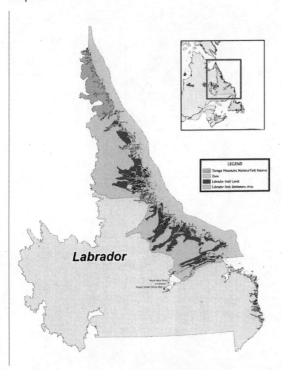

of the nineteenth century, almost all the Inuit had settled in the Moravian communities (Dorais, 2002: 142, 133; McMillan and Yellowhorn, 2004: 289). This voluntary transformation from nomadic to sedentary life, which occurred much earlier for the Inuit than the Innu, is in sharp contrast to the forced relocation of the Innu in the twentieth century. For the Innu, as described later in this chapter, the group's forced relocation and settlement greatly contributed to the development of many of the social, political, and economic problems that it faces today.

During the twentieth century, the Inuit became more dependent on the market economy of Canada. In addition to hunting and fishing, some Inuit began to participate in wage labour, especially after the construction of a military air base in central Labrador in 1941 (near Happy Valley–Goose Bay) and several radar sites along the coast after that. In 1949, Newfoundland and Labrador joined Confederation. Immediately

Map 2.3

following confederation, the federal and provincial governments negotiated a deal that stated that the federal government would provide
the province with money to cover its expenses as they related to the administration of the Labrador Inuit and Innu. By the end of the twentieth
century, almost all the Inuit were Christianized, educated in English
schools, and could speak the English language.

   In 1973, the Inuit formed the Labrador Inuit Association (LIA) "to
promote Inuit culture, improve the health and well-being of our people, protect our constitutional, democratic, and human rights, and
advance Labrador Inuit claims to our land and to self-government."
(Nunatsiavut Government, 2006b) The LIA, which was incorporated as
a non-profit organization under provincial law in 1975, was governed
by a twenty-one-member democratically elected board of directors,
representing the coastal Inuit communities of Nain (four members),

Makkovik (three), Postville (three), Rigolet (three), and Hopedale (three), and the inland communities in Happy Valley–Goose Bay (two) and North West River (one). The LIA also had a president and a vice-president, both of whom were directly elected by the Inuit. Board members had to be residents of the communities they represented, while all Inuit were eligible to run for the president and vice-president positions.

The LIA quickly became an important advocate for the Labrador Inuit, establishing a number of vital organizations such as the Labrador Inuit Development Corporation, the Labrador Inuit Health Commission, and the Torngasok Cultural Centre (Baikie, 1990; Nunatsiavut Government, 2006b). In addition to providing a variety of services and programs, the LIA was also responsible for negotiating a comprehensive land claims agreement with the federal and provincial governments (Haysom, 1990). After the LIA successfully negotiated a treaty in 2005, it was dissolved and replaced by the Nunatsiavut government.

The size of the Inuit population in Labrador is somewhere between 2436 (Statistics Canada, 2001) and 5300 (Nunatsiavut Government, 2006c).[1] The latter figure includes those of Inuit-only descent and *Kablunângajuit*, people of Inuit and European ancestry.

A Brief History of the Innu

Despite having a similar name, the Labrador Innu, also known as Montagnais, are a distinct Aboriginal group. The Innu were a nomadic hunting culture, travelling throughout the interiors of what is now Quebec and Labrador in the winter to hunt, and migrating to the coast of Labrador in the summer to fish (Matthews et al., 2006). Historically, Innu society generally emphasized individual freedom balanced with mutual responsibility. Authority, for the most part, was decentralized and dispersed among families and groups. Gender relations were non-hierarchical and egalitarian, with both genders having different spheres of responsibility (Samson, Wilson, and Mazower, 1999: 11–13). Most Innu organized themselves into lodge groups, which were three or four families of fifteen to twenty individuals living and travelling together. These lodge groups relied on consensus to make decisions, using effective orators to deliver their decisions to other groups when necessary.

Contact with European peoples first occurred with the Vikings one thousand years ago, then John Cabot in 1496, and thereafter a multitude of whalers, settlers, traders, and missionaries beginning with the Basque and ending with the French and English (Wadden, 1991: 26). The Innu remained relatively isolated from European settlement until the 1830s, when missionaries and traders began to set up permanent structures on Innu lands in Labrador. In 1916, the Hudson's Bay Company opened a permanent trading post at Davis Inlet and the Newfoundland government forcibly settled the Innu bands of Barren Ground and Davis Inlet there (Henriksen, 1981: 666).[2] Over time, these Innu members became dependent on European goods from the trading post (Backhouse and McRae, 2002: 12). In 1927, the border between Quebec and Labrador was created, dividing the Innu and their traditional lands in two. This action created two distinct Innu groups: the Innu in Quebec and the Innu in Labrador (Samson, Wilson, and Mazower, 1999: 15).

By the middle of the twentieth century, the Innu were heavily involved in the fur trade and were becoming increasingly exposed to missionary activities and sustained contact with non-Aboriginal peoples. In 1941, the government built a military airbase on Innu lands in central Labrador, which eventually spawned the city of Happy Valley–Goose Bay. In 1949, Newfoundland and Labrador joined Confederation. Shortly thereafter, the federal and provincial governments negotiated an agreement in which the federal government agreed to assume two-thirds of the costs associated with capital expenditures (welfare, health, and education) for the Labrador Inuit and 100 per cent of the costs for the Labrador Innu for a period of ten years. They also agreed to cover all costs associated with Inuit and Innu hospital treatment and to fund an aggressive anti-tuberculosis campaign. In exchange, the provincial government agreed to "assume all other financial and administrative responsibilities for the Indian and Eskimo population of Labrador excluding such federal benefits as family allowances and old age pensions" (Backhouse and McRae, 2002: 13). In 1964 the federal and provincial governments renewed this agreement with regard to health care costs and included a new provision under which the federal government agreed to provide up to $1 million per year for the provincial government's Innu- and Inuit-related expenses. Subsequent agreements extended these previous agreements with some minor modifications relating to the amount of money provided, the range of things that the money could be spent on, and how the money was paid and accounted for (ibid.: 13–14).

These federal-provincial spending arrangements had a dramatic effect on the Innu. Although historically the federal government provided most of the funding for programs and services for the Labrador Innu, the provincial government was largely responsible for spending those funds. Some analysts argue that the provincial government deliberately underfunded the Innu in the first two decades following Confederation, which in turn aggravated the Innu's domestic problems. As well, in the late 1950s and the late 1960s, respectively, the provincial government relocated the Innu to Sheshatshiu and to Davis Inlet II. Government officials forcibly settled the Innu in these two communities because caribou populations and fur prices had dropped dramatically during these decades; in the government's view, the Innu could no longer survive solely on hunting and trapping. More importantly, the government saw sedentarization (the settling of a nomadic culture) as a means to remove the Innu from lands that it believed had vast potential for economic development (Samson, Wilson, and Mazower, 1999: 16–17). The overall effect of government efforts to settle the Innu was to turn an Aboriginal group that had functioned quite well as a nomadic society into a dysfunctional settled one. Observers and the Innu themselves agree that the many domestic problems that they currently face, such as alcoholism, drug abuse, greed, and unemployment, are a result of government actions to settle and "civilize" them during the latter half of the twentieth century (Andrew, 2006; Ashini, 2006; Innu Nation, 1995; Michel, 2006; Samson, Wilson, and Mazower, 1999; Wadden, 1991). Many of these problems, as will be discussed below, have hindered the Innu from forging sufficient internal cohesion and fostering positive government perceptions of themselves to help them complete a modern treaty.

In December 2002 the federal government moved the Innu from Davis Inlet II to Natuashish, a new $200 million community that it had built for them. A month earlier, both communities became Indian bands under the Indian Act, meaning that, among other things, all their members were registered as status Indians. Despite these positive developments, some observers suggest that the problems that the Innu experienced at Davis Inlet II have followed them to Natuashish (CBC, 2005a).

Today, the majority of Innu live in Sheshatshiu (about an hour's drive west of Happy Valley–Goose Bay) and Natuashish (on the coast of Labrador in Sango Bay just south of Nain), with some members living in Happy Valley–Goose Bay. The Labrador Innu are represented by the Innu Nation at the modern treaty negotiating table. Innu Nation officials are elected to represent and serve the interests of members from both communities. A common practice has been for the Innu Nation president and the vice-president positions to be held by one member from each community. This practice is also true for comprehensive land claims negotiations; both communities regularly send one negotiator to serve on the Innu Nation negotiating team.

According to Canadian census data, the Innu population grew from 1404 in 1996 to 1714 in 2001. By July 2004, the Innu population had grown to 2100, with 700 members in Natuashish and 1400 in Sheshat-shiu (INAC, 2004).

The Labrador Inuit Journey

In 1977 the Labrador Inuit Association, on behalf of the Inuit of Labrador, submitted their land claim, *Our Footprints Our Everywhere*, to the federal and provincial governments for active negotiations. The land claim detailed the Inuit's use and occupation of their traditional lands since time immemorial. The federal government accepted the claim, praising it as "a model for other claim submissions by native peoples in Canada" (DIAND, 1990; see also Hawco, 2006). It was well researched, accurate, and comprehensive in outlining the Inuit claim (Hawco, 2006). The province, however, initially balked at the claim, mainly because then premier Frank Moores refused to acknowledge that Aboriginal peoples in his province were worthy of special recognition. According to Backhouse and McRae (2002), "The Province had historically taken the position that there was nothing to negotiate, that the Innu [and the Inuit] had no more claim to land than other Newfoundland residents" (ibid.: 41).

In March 1979 Brian Peckford of the Progressive Conservative Party became premier of Newfoundland and Labrador. His victory was important because he was more open to recognizing Inuit and Innu land claims than his predecessor (Rowell, 2006). In 1980 he decided to accept the Inuit claim for negotiations subject to two preconditions: negotiations had to lead to extinguishment, and the federal and provincial governments had to come to an agreement about cost sharing (Borlase, 1993: 310; Haysom, 2006; Haysom, 1990). These preconditions were problematic for two reasons. First, LIA leaders believed that a land claims agreement had to recognize Inuit rights, not extinguish them. Second, the issue of cost sharing was highly contentious, as demonstrated by the lack of a resolution until 1997.

Despite significant interest from the LIA, no active negotiations occurred until 1985. The reason was that until 1990, the federal government had a policy of actively negotiating with no more than six claimant groups at one time (Haysom, 2006; Haysom, 1990; Rowell, 2006). In June 1984 the federal and Inuit negotiators in the western Arctic signed the Inuvialuit agreement, opening up a spot on the active negotiations list. In that same year, federal officials invited the LIA to begin active comprehensive land claims negotiations. In 1985, however, the federal government announced it was suspending all CLC negotiations while it undertook a review of its comprehensive land claims policy. After the publication of the Coolican report,[3] the federal government made a number of important changes to its comprehensive land claims policy in 1986 (Graham, 1987: 255–6). Shortly thereafter, the province announced that it was going to review the Coolican report and the new federal policy and generate its own in response (Abele, 1986; Haysom, 1990, 2006). After completing its response, the province announced in October 1988 that despite the failure to achieve a cost-sharing agreement with the federal government, it was willing to begin tripartite negotiations. Framework agreement negotiations finally began in January 1989 and were completed in March 1990 (Chesley Andersen, 2006; Haysom, 2006; Rowell, 2006).

Although the framework agreement was completed relatively quickly, agreement-in-principle (AIP) negotiations would drag on for approximately nine years. The first six years (1990–6) of AIP negotiations were extremely slow and unproductive for a number of reasons. First, the federal and provincial governments were at an impasse over cost sharing. The province's "position was that it would contribute to the negotiations what it had the capacity to contribute which were matters within provincial jurisdiction … including land, renewable and non-renewable resources, etc." (Carter, 2006). The province also felt that it was under no obligation to contribute money to the agreement. The federal government, by contrast, wanted the province to pay for some of the costs of the agreement because it did not want to set a precedent of exempting other provinces from cost sharing. One anonymous interviewee mentioned that the outstanding claims in British Columbia were in the back of the federal government's mind throughout cost-sharing negotiations with the Newfoundland government.

Second, the province was simply unprepared to negotiate an AIP because it had never done so before. It did not have the necessary experience and knowledge to properly negotiate an AIP. Third, there was a lack of political will at the provincial level. Although Liberal premier Clyde Wells wanted a deal, it was not one of his main priorities (Marshall, 2006), partly because he did not believe in special recognition for collectivities (Innes, 2006). The result was that provincial negotiators did not have a clear mandate at the negotiating table (Marshall, 2006). Time and time again, they would have to go back to their superiors for instructions, resulting in slow progress at the negotiating table (Pain, 2006; Rowell, 2006). According to Veryan Haysom (2006), lawyer and LIA negotiator, "A large part of the problem was that provincial policy at the time was very limited and restrictive and the Inuit were nego-tiating despite that policy, not under it. It was largely this that forced provincial negotiators to seek mandate changes at the policy level." Fi-nally, the federal government adopted a passive stance at the negotiat-ing table on the basis that most of the issues under negotiation involved provincial jurisdiction. Throughout much of the negotiations, it pre-ferred to let the LIA and the province negotiate while it lurked in the background. Only when the province and the LIA would come to an agreement on a particular issue would the federal government take an active role. Federal negotiators would take the tentative LIA-provincial agreement to their superiors and return with demands that had to be accommodated through further negotiations (Haysom, 2006; Marshall, 2006; Pain, 2006; Rowell, 2006).

Voisey's Bay and a New Premier

By 1996, six years of negotiations had generated one initialled chapter (eligibility and enrolment) and some progress on other matters (Carter, 2006; Pain, 2006). The pace of negotiations quickly changed as a result of two events. The first was the discovery of a massive nickel deposit in Voisey's Bay, a region between Nain and Natuashish that both the Innu and the Inuit had previously claimed (Jararuse, 2006; Michel, 2006; Riche, 2006). The discovery of nickel created a huge mineral rush in Labrador, and both levels of government were enthusiastic about accelerating land claims negotiations to clear the way for mineral ex-ploration and extraction in the area (Haysom, 2006; Innes, 2006; Shafto, 2006). This enthusiasm was especially true of the provincial govern-ment, which saw the discovery as a crucial opportunity to increase its economic wealth.

The second event that had a significant impact on both sets of ne-gotiations was the election of Brian Tobin as premier of Newfound-land and Labrador in January 1996. Tobin brought his federal-level experience to the table and made settling the claims a priority for his government. He set out clear parameters for each of the items under

negotiation, ratified them in cabinet, and authorized provincial negotiators to get a deal done using those parameters (Marshall, 2006). According to LIA and provincial officials, the election of Tobin was a real
opportunity to make significant progress towards an AIP (Chesley Andersen, 2006; Barbour, 2006; Hawco, 2006; Haysom 2006; Marshall 2006;
Warren 2006). Some officials have indicated, however, that although
Tobin clearly energized the process, his interest in treaty negotiations
was conditioned strongly by the economic potential of Voisey's Bay.

Initially, Voisey's Bay was an obstacle to Inuit negotiations. By the
spring of 1996, Inuit negotiations had stalled (Carter, 2006; Pain, 2006)
and become strained due to personality conflicts between some government and Inuit negotiators. As well, a number of issues, such as the
amount of total land to be included in the agreement, resource revenue
sharing, and self-government, remained unresolved. The most important obstacle, however, was the certainty and finality provision, with
the Inuit extremely reluctant to adopt the cede, release, and surrender provision found in other modern treaties across Canada. The Inuit
negotiating team, which included Toby Andersen, Isabelle Pain, Judy
Rowell, and Veryan Haysom, had become frustrated with the federal
negotiator and asked the federal government to bring in an external
negotiator to represent the federal government. The federal government refused. The discovery of nickel in Voisey's Bay exacerbated this
conflictual environment. Both the Inuit and the Innu had claimed the
Voisey's Bay area before the nickel deposit discovery. Once nickel was
discovered in the area, the federal and provincial governments pulled
Voisey's Bay off the negotiating table and encouraged Inco to initiate
mining operations. In response, the Innu and the Inuit conducted joint
protests in the area and applied for (and received on appeal) a court injunction to stop development.

Although by 1996 negotiations with the LIA had stalled, the pace of
negotiations changed after the Newfoundland Court of Appeal handed
down its injunction. The pace changed because the injunction had the
potential to prevent the federal and provincial governments from developing, and reaping significant economic benefits from, the nickel deposit. In the fall of 1996, the federal and provincial governments and the
Inuit agreed to fast-track negotiations through the use of intensive and
frequent negotiation sessions. The federal government also acceded to
the LIA's request for a new negotiator by appointing Jim Mackenzie,
a law professor from Carleton University, as chief federal negotiator.
Although the parties made substantial progress during fast-tracked

negotiations, a number of critical issues remained unresolved: the amount of total land to be included in the agreement, resource revenue sharing, Inuit participation in economic development, financial compensation, self-government, and the nature and composition of the national park and settlement areas.

In October 1997 the three parties agreed to hold a three-day senior officials meeting in Ottawa to resolve these issues. On the federal side, the deputy minister of INAC, Scott Serson, was brought in to sit beside the federal negotiator to ensure the critical issues were resolved. Although Serson did have a number of cabinet-established bottom lines that he could not cross, he had significant latitude to negotiate and create new and innovative policies to resolve the impasse. In short, he had the mandate to get a deal done, mainly because the general feeling within the federal bureaucracy and within cabinet was that there was a need to show that "Gathering Strength"[4] could successfully address the issues raised by the Royal Commission on Aboriginal Peoples (Serson, 2006). On the provincial side, Premier Brian Tobin appointed Harold Marshall, a senior provincial civil servant, and Bill Rowat, a former federal civil servant, to sit beside the provincial negotiators with a mandate to resolve the critical issues. Marshall's role was to act as the voice of the premier at the table. Rowat provided his expertise and knowledge of the federal bureaucracy. To give added weight to the premier's commitment to push LIA negotiations forward, Tobin and the member of the Provincial House of Assembly for the riding encompassing the Inuit communities, Wally Andersen, stayed at the Chateau Laurier hotel during the meetings to provide on-call advice and immediate decision making.

On the Inuit side, the Inuit negotiators, who had remained virtually the same since 1989, remained at the table, with the addition of Chesley Andersen, a former Inuit Tapiriit Kanatami representative and employee who had previous experience working across the table from Scott Serson during the constitutional rounds. The LIA team also had immediate access to the LIA president, vice-president, and board members by phone anytime they needed to make immediate and crucial decisions. Three days of negotiations stretched into eleven, and on 28 October 1997 the three parties signed a three-page agreement resolving the major issues of contention (the total amount of land to be included in the agreement, resource revenue sharing, Inuit participation in development, financial compensation, self-government, cost sharing, and the national park and settlement areas). From there, negotiations moved quickly to an initialled AIP in 1999 and a successful ratification vote on the AIP on 25 June 2001. On that day, 76 per cent of eligible Inuit voted to ratify the AIP, with a turnout of 85 per cent.[5] Highlights of the ratified AIP (Indian and Northern Affairs Canada, 2001) include the following:

- Preamble: the Parties recognize the Inuit's claim to the Labrador Inuit Land Claims Area based on the Inuit's traditional and current occupation and usage of said lands;
- General Provisions: the AIP is a non–legally binding document. The final agreement will be protected under s. 35 of the *Constitution Act, 1982* and Labrador Inuit will continue to have Canadian citizenship. The Charter of Rights will apply to the Inuit government;
- Lands: Land selection will occur during final agreement negotiations.
- Settlements Lands: The settlement area will include 28,000 square miles (72,520 square kilometers) of lands and 17,000 square miles (44,030 square kilometers) of adjacent ocean. 3,000 square miles will be put aside for the Torngat Mountains National Park Reserve;
- Inuit Lands: Labrador Inuit will receive special rights to 6,100 square miles (15,800 square kilometers), including the ability to make laws regulating and managing those lands in a variety of ways;
- Non-Renewable Resources: The Inuit government is to receive 50% of the first $2 million of revenue, plus 5% of any additional provincial revenues from settlement lands that are outside of Inuit lands. For Inuit lands, the Inuit are to receive 25% of provincial revenues from subsurface resources and exclusive right to the carving stone and ownership of 1,525 square miles (3,950 square kilometers) of Specified Material Lands;
- Voisey's Bay Project: the Inuit will receive 3% of provincial revenues from the mineral resources extracted from Voisey's Bay. Other terms related to Voisey's Bay will be negotiated before the final agreement;
- Water: Inuit can use water in the settlement area for personal and domestic purposes without a permit. The Inuit government and the province have the authority to jointly issue licenses in Inuit lands;
- Ocean Management: Marine management and development requires consultation with the Inuit government;
- Economic Development: Developers must negotiate IBAs with the Inuit before engaging in development on Inuit lands. The federal government agrees to give equal consideration to Labrador Inuit

businesses when contracting and commit to a representative public service in the settlement area;

- National Parks and Protected Areas: The Inuit government shall establish a national park in the Torngat Mountains and can create additional protected areas in Inuit lands;
- Land Use Planning: the provincial and Inuit governments will establish a steering committee to formulate a comprehensive land use plan for the settlement area;
- Environmental Assessment: Crown assessment laws remain in effect on settlement lands. The Inuit government can pass environmental assessment laws regulating Inuit lands;
- Wildlife and Plants: Labrador Inuit will be able to harvest wildlife and plants throughout the settlement area although such activities will be subject to a variety of federal and provincial laws relating to conservation, public health, public safety, and international obligations;
- Fisheries: Labrador Inuit will be able to fish for subsistence purposes throughout the settlement area. A joint fisheries board will make recommendations on the management of the fisheries in the settlement area. The federal minister, however, will have final authority over the management of the fisheries;
- Self-Government: Details of the Inuit constitution, governance structures, and powers are described here;
- Fiscal Financing Agreements: The Inuit will continue to receive federal and provincial programs and services. A funding agreement will be negotiated every five years;
- Capital Transfers: The federal government will pay the Inuit $140 million according to a payment schedule to be set during final agreement negotiations. This money will be held in trust for all beneficiaries and will be used to pay any outstanding negotiation loans;
- Taxation: Federal and provincial taxation laws will continue to apply. The Inuit government can also directly tax Inuit living on Inuit lands and in Inuit communities;
- Eligibility and Enrolment: Criteria will be similar to those for membership in the Labrador Inuit Association;
- Ratification of the Final Agreement: A majority of eligible voters must vote in favour of the final agreement;
- Implementation: Canada will provide $115 million to the Inuit government to help with the implementation of the final agreement.

With a completed AIP in hand, final agreement negotiations progressed relatively quickly, but not without some significant problems.
According to federal, provincial, and LIA negotiators, two issues were
particularly difficult to resolve. The first was land selection, the process in which the parties decided the lands over which the Aboriginal
groups received formal ownership within the overall area covered by
the land claims agreement. The Inuit were asked to provide a preliminary land selection proposal and present it to the governments for their
consideration. The provincial reaction to the Inuit preliminary proposal
was quite negative. Back in 1994, the province had offered seven small
rectangular blocks of land to the Inuit. The Inuit, however, proposed to
select a series of large "ribbons" along waterways and along much of
the coastline of Labrador. According to one interviewee, then-premier
Brian Tobin remarked something to the effect that if he accepted the
Inuit proposal, he would need a parachute to get into Labrador. In other
words, Tobin was unhappy with the fact that the Inuit were claiming
all of the desirable lands adjacent to water bodies and the ocean in the
northern part of Labrador. Despite this initial reaction, the LIA and the
province were able to come to an agreement. The Inuit ended up accepting some land that they were not really interested in, and giving up
some land that they originally wanted. The province eventually com-
promised by accepting the Inuit "ribbon" concept and giving up more
of the coastline than it had originally wanted.

A second issue that caused some difficulty during final agreement
negotiations was Voisey's Bay. The initialled AIP had originally stated
that the Voisey's Bay chapter would be negotiated during final agreement negotiations. However, Inco was ready to proceed ahead of schedule and the governments were anxious to move the project forward
before completing a final agreement.[6] The Inuit eventually agreed to let
the project go forward, mainly because of their confidence in a suite of
three Voisey's Bay agreements that they had signed,[7] as well as an informal understanding between the LIA president, premier, and federal
minister of INAC that the land claims agreement would be completed
if Voisey's Bay moved forward.

The Final Agreement was initialled by the parties in 2004. Before
the federal and provincial governments ratified the agreement in their
respective legislatures, the LIA held a ratification referendum. On 26
May 2004, 76.4 per cent of Inuit voters voted yes to ratification, with a
voter turnout of 86.5 per cent. Those who did not vote were counted as
voting "no" to ratifying the agreement.[8] Of those who voted, support

for the agreement was quite strong in the five coastal communities. In Nain, for instance, 96.6% of residents supported the final agreement, 97.9% in Hopedale, 92.2% in Makkovik, 95.9% in Postville, and 87.6% in Rigolet. Support was less enthusiastic in the two main urban centres in the interior of Labrador. Only 76.6% of North West River residents and 77.9% of Happy Valley–Goose Bay residents supported the final agreement (LIA, 2004: 3). These results were probably weaker because their communities' lands were not included as part of the Labrador Inuit Lands or the Labrador Inuit Settlement Lands. Rather, they were designated as special areas to which the Inuit would have only limited rights (Labrador Inuit Land Claims Agreement, 2005; Hibbs, 2006).

Once the LIA completed its ratification of the agreement, the province and the federal government passed settlement legislation in their respective houses in 2004. Finally, after twenty-eight years of negotiations, federal, provincial, and Inuit leaders formally signed the Labrador Inuit Final Agreement on 22 January 2005 in Nain, Labrador. It would come into effect shortly thereafter.

In terms of the treaty's contents, key provisions include:

- the creation of 72,520 square kilometres of land called "Labrador Inuit Settlement Lands," of which 15,799 is designated as "Labrador Inuit Lands": Labrador Inuit Settlement Lands are lands over which the federal, provincial, and Nunatsiavut governments are to share jurisdiction. Labrador Inuit Lands, by contrast, are lands that the Labrador Inuit hold stronger interests in, including a 25 per cent interest in subsurface resources.
- a cash settlement of $140 million (1997 dollars) over fifteen years plus a one-time payment of $156 million to assist with implementation
- a fifteen-year repayment schedule for $51 million in loans provided by the federal government to the LIA to negotiate the treaty
- water management and water usage rights
- ocean management rights: Inuit have the right to be consulted before any ocean management plans are created.
- economic development: the Nunatsiavut government and interested developers must negotiate an impact and benefits agreement for projects involving Labrador Inuit Lands and Labrador Inuit Settlement Lands.
- national parks: creation of the Torngat Mountains National Park Reserve in Northern Labrador

- land use planning for Labrador Inuit Settlement Lands: to be done bilaterally by the Nunatsiavut and provincial governments.
- Voisey's Bay: Resource revenue sharing and each party's interests in the area are clarified – the Inuit are to receive 5 per cent of provincial revenues derived from the subsurface resources extracted from the Voisey's Bay Area.
- environmental assessment: Federal and provincial laws are paramount over Nunatsiavut laws in cases of conflict over environmental assessment.
- Inuit harvesting rights in wildlife and plants: Inuit can harvest wildlife and plants for food, social, and ceremonial purposes. The agreement also calls for the creation of a co-management board for administering and protecting wildlife and plants in the settlement area.
- Inuit harvesting rights in fish and marine mammals: They can harvest these products for food, social, and ceremonial purposes. The agreement also calls for the creation of a fisheries co-management board.
- archaeological rights: sole control over archaeological activity in Labrador Inuit Lands belongs to the Nunatsiavut government, while the federal government maintains control over archaeological activity in the Labrador Inuit Settlement Area.
- Labrador Inuit self-government: This includes provisions regarding an Inuit constitution, community governments, Inuit courts, Inuit law enforcement officers, and jurisdiction over a variety of powers and programs.
- fiscal financing arrangements: Labrador Inuit continue to be eligible for federal and provincial programs and services and can negotiate with the federal and provincial governments every five years regarding funding for agreed-upon Inuit programs and services.
- taxation: Labrador Inuit remain subject to federal and provincial taxation laws. The Nunatsiavut government and its community governments may directly tax Labrador Inuit and can negotiate with the Crown to tax non-Inuit peoples on Inuit lands.
- dispute resolution (Labrador Inuit Land Claims Agreement, 2005)

Broadly speaking, the Labrador Inuit Final Agreement is somewhat similar to agreements signed by other Aboriginal groups in Canada. In one sense, it is difficult to compare agreements because each agreement is designed to address the specific needs of each Aboriginal group. Nonetheless, all comprehensive land claims agreements tend to cover the same types of issues such as permanently clarifying owner- ship of settlement and non-settlement lands (certainty and finality), the amount of total land to be included in the agreement (land quantum), land use planning, fish and wildlife, migratory birds, water manage- ment and usage rights, ocean management, history/culture/archaeol- ogy, economic development, eligibility and enrolment, and fisheries, among others.

In terms of the Labrador Inuit Final Agreement, there are two minor differences worth pointing out. First, the certainty provision is different in that it states that the Labrador Inuit "cede and release" their Aborigi- nal rights to their lands, as opposed to "cede, release, and surrender." This provision is described in greater detail below. Second, the Final Agreement includes a self-government chapter within its text. Most other comprehensive land claims agreements in Canada contain a self- government chapter that only set out the terms under which a separate self-government agreement would be negotiated. In this case, the Lab- rador Inuit have included their self-government agreement within the text of the Final Agreement, which they believe strengthens the consti- tutional status of their right to self-government.

The Labrador Innu Journey

In 1977 the Naskapi Montagnais Innu Association on behalf of the Innu in Sheshatshiu and Davis Inlet submitted its land claim to the federal and provincial governments. The federal government conditionally ac- cepted the claim in 1978, requiring that the Innu submit an acceptable – according to Western standards of geography, anthropology, history, and archaeology – land use and occupancy study before negotiations could begin. Unlike the Labrador Inuit, whose claim was accepted for negotiations in 1979–80, it would not be until 1991 that the Innu Nation, the organization that replaced the Naskapi Montagnais Innu Associa- tion as the association representing the Labrador Innu, would submit a study that was acceptable to the federal government (Innu Nation, 1998; Pelley, 2006). There were numerous reasons for this delay. One was that the Innu Nation initially lacked adequate expertise and resources to produce such a document (John-Pierre Ashini, 2006; Hawco, 2006; Nui, 2006; Pelley, 2006; Riche, 2006). Another was that during the 1980s, the Innu held a notion of sovereignty that was incompatible with Cana- dian notions (Hawco, 2006; Pelley, 2006). In essence (and as explained in more detail below), government and Innu negotiators held opposing views regarding whether a land claims agreement should lead to the cession, release, and surrender of Aboriginal title. There was also a strong view in the community that protesting, pursuing litigation, and seeking international recognition were more effective strategies than negotiating for achieving Innu goals (Innu Nation, 1995; Innu Nation, 1998). This preference for confrontational tactics was partly the result of the Innu's interactions and experiences with state agencies. Specifically, government unilateral actions on Innu lands created intense hostility among Innu peoples towards both levels of government. Finally, the Innu communities were suffering from a wide range of social and economic problems that would paralyse any type of collective action towards negotiations (Backhouse and McRae, 2002).

From 1977 to 1991 the Innu communities and the Innu Nation focused on political lobbying and protests. In particular, they protested low-level flying over their lands and petitioned the United Nations to pressure the Canadian government to recognize their rights (Alcantara, 2010). These tactics were supported by the Innu communities. In 1987 Innu Nation held community consultations on whether to begin negotiations under the CLC process, but the communities decided to continue protesting rather than negotiate. At the same time, the Innu communities continued to suffer from a number of domestic ailments, including high unemployment, a low standard of living, lack of basic services and goods, and high levels of alcohol, drug, physical, and sexual abuse, much of which stemmed from their forced transition from nomadic to settled life beginning in the late 1950s (Hawco, 2006; Innu Nation, 1995; Innu Nation, 1998).

The 1990s would see their focus slowly shift from nothing but protests to a mixture of protests and negotiations. They continued to protest and lobby against low-level flying during this period (Alcantara, 2010), but leaders in Sheshatshiu started to become more interested in negotiating due to the mixed results of protesting. In 1991 Innu Nation decided on the basis of community consultations to begin negotiations with the federal government under the comprehensive land claims process. However, severe domestic, social, and economic problems in Sheshatshiu and Davis Inlet would force the Innu to shift their focus away from negotiations to generating solutions to these specific problems, all of which were highlighted by suddenly interested domestic and international media (Innu Nation, 1995; Innu Nation, 1998; Wadden, 1991).

Another factor delaying Innu negotiations was political turmoil. Leadership was constantly changing and rival factions were emerging along family lines. Since the early 1980s, but especially in the 1990s, Innu leaders have held divergent views regarding whether to negotiate, with one faction focusing on negotiation and compromise within the Canadian framework, and the other on the recognition of Innu sovereignty over all their traditional lands (Hawco, 2006; Marshall, 2006; Michel, 2006; Paul Rich, 2006). Some have remarked that there is a clear divide between the younger, more formally educated leaders, and the less educated and more traditional leaders, with the former being more interested in treaties and the latter more against it. This divergence may be the result of these leaders having different experiences and interactions with the agencies (i.e., the education system, Department of Indian Affairs and Northern Development) of the Canadian state.

Significant progress was made with the election of Peter Penashue as the president of Innu Nation in 1990.[9] Penashue, a pragmatist, was committed to negotiating an agreement that would empower the Innu to solve their internal problems, protect their traditional ways and practices, and allow them to reap the benefits of the economic development potential of their lands. Negotiations between Innu Nation, the federal government, and the province began in July 1991, but progressed slowly as the Innu communities struggled with internal problems and further disputes with the federal and provincial governments over their illegal use of Innu traditional lands.

In 1994, as mentioned above, a large nickel deposit was found in Voisey's Bay, an area that the Innu had included in their original land claim. Both governments, but especially the province, became very interested in settling the Innu land claim to facilitate the development of the area. Framework agreement negotiations, which had been on and off from 1992 to 1995, resumed full time in May 1995. In October 1995, the three parties were able to initial a framework agreement, which was then ratified by the Innu in a community vote on 22 January 1996 (Indian and Northern Affairs Canada, 1996).[10]

Since then, however, AIP negotiations, always the most difficult in land claims negotiations, have been slow, with limited progress. In 1999 federal officials suspended negotiations with the Innu Nation due to what it saw as unreasonable Innu demands. According to federal officials, "The suspension of the negotiations in 2000 was necessary ... because the Innu claim was not in their [federal officials'] view a serious claim. It was simply made up of the best element[s] of every land claim negotiated by Aboriginal people across the country and was 'out of the ball park'" (Backhouse and McRae, 2002: 41).[11] In addition to suspending active negotiations, the federal government stopped providing Innu Nation with negotiation funding. Once negotiations resumed in 2001, the federal government restored negotiation funding to the Innu, but at a significantly lower level (ibid.: 41).

The federal government restarted negotiations in 2001 because Innu Nation submitted a new land claims package which the federal government believed was much more reasonable than the previous one. Shortly thereafter, the parties negotiated a memorandum of understanding (MOU) and an impact and benefits agreement (IBA) for the Voisey's Bay area.[12] With the MOU and IBA in hand, progress on the Innu land claims AIP slowed considerably, with negotiations stalling over the amount of total land to be included in the agreement, the exact powers to be included in the self-government chapter, and, most importantly, the nature of the certainty provision (Nui, 2006; Riche, 2006).

In May 2006, negotiations accelerated when Premier Danny Williams announced that his provincial government was taking control over the multi-billion-dollar Lower Churchill hydroelectric development project in Labrador. After reviewing the tendered proposals from private companies, Premier Williams concluded that "it became clear that a Newfoundland and Labrador–led development presented the best option to realize our objective to develop this tremendous, clean source of renewable energy" (Government of Newfoundland and Labrador, 2006). A major obstacle to his plans, however, was the outstanding Innu land claim, which involved the lands on which the development was to be built. Immediately after the premier's press conference, Innu Nation vice-president Peter Penashue warned that Innu consent would only be given if the province provided financial compensation for the Upper Churchill project, signed an IBA with the Innu for the Lower Churchill project, and completed the Innu's land claims AIP.

In response to these demands, the province initiated special negotiations with Innu Nation to achieve Innu consent. The result of these negotiations was the "Tshash Petapen Agreement," otherwise known as the "New Dawn Agreement" (NDA), signed by the government of Newfoundland and Labrador, the Energy Corporation of Newfoundland and Labrador, and Innu Nation on 26 September 2008. The NDA, in essence, was a framework agreement designed to help the parties complete a land claims AIP, an IBA for the Lower Churchill development, and a financial compensation agreement for the Upper Churchill hydroelectric development. With respect to the AIP, the parties agreed to the amount and specific parcels of land to be transferred to the Innu. For instance, the parties agreed that the Innu would receive 5000 square miles of Category One Land (Innu Lands), 9000 square miles of Category Two Land (Settlement Lands), and 13,000 square miles of Category Three Land (lands to which Innu have limited harvesting rights for migratory species of wildlife). The agreement also specified that the Innu would have the right to negotiate future IBAs for certain parcels of land designated as economic development areas, and be able to better indicate their land selection preferences for four other parcels. In addition to these AIP provisions, the New Dawn Agreement also set the framework for negotiating a Lower Churchill IBA and a final agreement on financial compensation for the Upper Churchill project. In terms of the former agreement, the parties agreed that the Innu could negotiate to receive up to $2 million a year in compensation until 2041, at which point they would receive a percentage of the project's revenue. In terms of the latter agreement, Innu Nation was given the choice between 5 per cent of net project revenue or $5 million per year payable once the project began producing commercial power. Finally, section 4 of the New Dawn Agreement stated that if the parties failed to ratify and execute any one of these three agreements on or before 31 January 2009, none of them would come into effect.

Although public reaction to the New Dawn Agreement was generally positive, news reports suggest that at least some Innu band members were less enthusiastic. Former Innu Nation president David Nuk was upset that there was little consultation[13] before the signing of the agreement, which still has to be ratified by the Innu communities. "It's going to be hard for the leadership to sell this project to the communities, I think ... What's the point of voting on something that's been, in my opinion, been done? There was a lack of consultation and [people were] undermined by this procedure." Greg Patishi, an Innu member who lives in Sheshatshiu, agreed, stating the first time he heard about the agreement was on the radio. "I'm still shocked ... In some ways, you feel left out. Again, hopefully it would be nice for them to tell us what's going on" (CBC, 2008). Nonetheless, several current Innu Nation politicians and civil servants indicate that there is significant community support emerging in favour of the New Dawn Agreement. They attribute much of this support as coming from Innu youth, who seem to be more pro-development and who also represent approximately three-quarters of the Nation's entire membership. As well, recent leadership changes have produced a set of leaders who are much more pro-development than in the past. As of September 2009, however, neither the New Dawn Agreement nor the three agreements described above have been negotiated, or ratified and enacted.

Economic Development: A Necessary Condition?

Would the Inuit have completed their treaty if Voisey's Bay had not been discovered? The evidence suggests yes, although the timeline for completion would have extended well beyond January 2005. It was clear from the outset that federal and provincial officials were willing, albeit at a slower pace, to settle the Inuit claim. The Inuit statement of claim in 1977 was praised by the federal government and later the provincial government as "a model for other claim submissions by native peoples in Canada" (DIAND 1990; Hawco 2006). After submitting its claim, the LIA was one of the first Aboriginal groups to have its claim accepted for active negotiations when one of the initial six groups[14] completed its agreement in 1984. Once active negotiations began in January 1989, the LIA was able to negotiate a framework agreement by March 1990. The period from 1990 to 1996 saw some progress, with one chapter initialled and advancement on other matters. Voisey's Bay did slow down negotiations initially, but a combination of factors unique to the Inuit resulted in the negotiations accelerating, leading to a completed treaty in 2005.

On the other hand, Innu negotiations showed very little promise for completion before, during, or after Voisey's Bay. Despite its submission around the same time as the Inuit, the Innu Nation statement of claim was not accepted until 1991, when the Innu Nation finally submitted a land use and occupancy study that was acceptable to the federal government. In 1996, the parties completed a framework agreement (mainly as a result of the efforts of Innu Nation president Peter Penashue and the fact that such agreements tend to be procedural rather than substantive), but since then AIP negotiations have seen little progress, stalling over self-government, the total amount of land covered by the agreement, land selection, economic development, hunting, fishing, and culture, and, most importantly, certainty and finality. Indeed, the federal and provincial governments have suspended negotiations several times in the hope that Innu negotiators would come to the table with more reasonable expectations and demands. Federal and provincial government officials have also preferred to work with the Innu on developing community healing and capacity building (that is, human and organizational resources and expertise) in advance of negotiating a land claims or self-government agreement (Backhouse and McRae, 2002). Over the last five years or so, Innu leaders have agreed to focus on community and government capacity building and have pursued a number of initiatives, such as gaining reserve status under the Indian Act, to accomplish these goals.

Factors Affecting Treaty Negotiation Outcomes

Compatibility of Goals

So what determines negotiation outcomes? More specifically, in light of the theoretical framework of this book and the experiences of the Innu and Inuit, what are the strategies that produce settlements and non-settlements? Table 2.1 summarizes the key factors. The first factor is the compatibility of government and Aboriginal goals. By compatible goals, I mean the matching of government and Aboriginal goals with respect to the purposes of a final agreement. Compatible goals were clearly present in the Labrador Inuit negotiations. For example, during final agreement negotiations over the certainty and finality provisions, federal officials were open to negotiating an alternative to the usual "cede, release, and surrender" provision, or using an alternative provision found in another agreement in Canada. LIA leaders and negotiators were unwilling to accept any provision that included the word "surrender," while the province insisted on the usual "cede, release, and surrender" provision. Despite these differences, the parties were able to come to an agreement, partly because federal and provincial policies evolved over time to become more flexible, but most importantly because Labrador Inuit leaders and culture value compromise and negotiation. The shared goal among the federal, provincial, and Inuit leaders and negotiators was to avoid future conflict, protests, and litigation by creating certainty in the lands that the Inuit had claimed. According to federal and Inuit sources, provincial officials benefited from federal and Inuit officials bringing their experiences and knowledge about treaties signed by other Aboriginal groups in Canada to the negotiating table. Specifically, the negotiating officials were able to draw upon experiences from other treaty negotiations to fashion a certainty provision that would be acceptable to all three parties. The key lesson from previous treaty negotiations was that flexibility in the

Table 2.1 Factors relative to the Aboriginal groups that affect which CLC negotiation outcomes are obtained

Factors promoting a successful outcome	Factors leading to an unsuccessful outcome
– Compatibility of government and Aboriginal group goals – Minimal use of confrontational tactics by the Aboriginal group – Strong Aboriginal group cohesion as it relates to the treaty process – Positive government perceptions of Aboriginal group capacity	– Incompatibility of government and Aboriginal group goals – More frequent use of confrontational tactics by the Aboriginal group – Weak Aboriginal group cohesion as it relates to the treaty process – Negative government perceptions of Aboriginal group capacity

certainty provision was possible, even if in the end the provision legally resulted in the same outcome (Alcantara, 2009).

In the end, the agreed-upon certainty provision satisfied all three parties. The Inuit were able to keep their Aboriginal rights in their Inuit Lands (their core lands), subject to the terms of the agreement. In exchange, they ceded and released (but did not surrender) their Aboriginal rights to Inuit Settlement Lands (lands over which all three parties have extensive shared jurisdiction) and all lands previously claimed by the Inuit that were not included in the treaty. According to a number of anonymous sources, the province accepted the "cede and release" provision because, in its view, the level of certainty generated by the words "cede" and "release" was sufficient for pursuing economic development in the lands affected by the treaty (see also Alcantara, 2009).

Contrast these experiences with the Innu case. The Innu negotiators originally came to the table with the notion that any agreement had to recognize Innu sovereignty over their traditional lands. Both the federal and the provincial governments, however, have refused to recognize Innu sovereignty (Andrew, 2006; Innes, 2006; Wadden, 1991: 200; Innu Nation, 1995: 175; Pelley, 2006). By the early 1990s, the Innu negotiators' use of the term "Innu sovereignty" during negotiations occurred much less frequently, culminating in a completed framework agreement in 1996.

Although the use of the concept of "Innu sovereignty" has largely disappeared at the negotiation table, it remains a powerful idea among some Innu leaders and community members. For instance, one community member has said that "the Innu should have total control on Innu Lands – no sharing of control with government" (Innu Nation, 1998: 44). A former Davis Inlet chief has remarked: "The Innu government should have full power in Innu lands" (Innu Nation, 1998: 44). Another member has said, "On the core lands, how are we going to manage the land if the government can still overturn Innu Government decisions?" (ibid.: 45). The persistence of ideas about Innu sovereignty at the community level has hindered the ability of negotiators to complete an agreement-in-principle. This persistence is problematic because Innu negotiators feel an obligation to undertake extensive public consultations with community members before any agreement can be signed. This obligation to negotiate stems from cultural norms, as opposed to be being tied to the notion of Innu sovereignty. As a result, negotiators are constantly torn between satisfying federal and provincial demands that an agreement not recognize Innu sovereignty and satisfying community demands for recognition and protection of Innu sovereignty. What makes the Innu case striking is the degree to which members and leaders are divided on whether or not to negotiate. Since formal negotiations began in 1990, two factions have emerged to support or oppose negotiations. These factions have, over time, become more conflictual with each other over land claims negotiations and other related issues. Some observers have mentioned that the conflicts have become intensely personal and extremely bitter. Just before his death, for instance, Innu Nation president Ben Michel spoke to me about how deeply divided Innu community leaders and members were over negotiations and other related spin-off benefits; others echoed his comments. Since his death, the anti-Michel faction, led by Peter Penashue, has taken control of Innu Nation. This development may shift the negotiation preferences of the Innu.

Tactics

In general, government officials prefer negotiations to other tactics because they perceive the costs (money, reputation, and political capital) of the alternatives (i.e., litigation, protests, and international lobbying) as being much higher. As a result, governments are more likely to work towards agreements with those Aboriginal groups that show a commitment to negotiations and that limit the use of confrontational tactics. Conversely, governments are less likely to work towards final agreements with those Aboriginal groups with whom they have a long history of confrontation.

Since 1977, Inuit leaders and negotiators have consistently used a strategy of compromise and negotiation. The strategies of protest, litigation, media, and courting recognition from international legal and political bodies were rarely considered or used by LIA presidents, vice-presidents, or board members (Andersen III, 2006; Tony Andersen, 2006; Barbour, 2006; Hibbs, 2006; Pain, 2006). All of the LIA politicians, board members, and negotiators whom I interviewed indicated that leaders, negotiators, and even community members were consistent over time in their desire for an agreement through negotiations as opposed to other approaches. For the Labrador Inuit, settling land claims and achieving self-government were central to empowering the Inuit to control their lives, their economy, and their health and cultural well-being (Andersen III, 2006; Tony Andersen, 2006; Barbour, 2006; Haysom, 1990). Their commitment to negotiations rather than using other tactics is partly a reflection of Inuit culture in general, which values consensus building and compromise over other tactics for resolving conflicts (see, for instance, Alfred, 2005: 122; McPherson, 2003: 129). Government actors recognized the Inuit's commitment to negotiating and were willing to work with the Inuit towards a completed treaty, even during difficult times and through difficult issues.

Contrast this with the Innu, who have in general tended to favour protesting, media campaigns, litigation, and courting recognition from international bodies. In the words of the Innu Nation's Davis Inlet Inquiry Commission, "Protests are a good way to get our voices heard. We need to use strong tactics, vocal speaking out against unwanted developments and in support of our rights ... We need to do this to get their [white people] support to help us fight governments. If other people understand our position, it will be good. We also need to lobby foreign governments on our human rights" (Innu Nation, 1995: 179). For much of their involvement in the CLC process, Innu leaders, negotiators, and community members have engaged in confrontational strategies, fighting the federal and provincial governments over hunting regulations, military flights over their land, poor administration of police and judicial services, lack of resources to combat domestic ills, unemployment, and poor housing, rather than negotiating (see, for instance, Nuke, 2006; Michel, 2006; CBC, 1999; CBC, 2000a; CBC, 2000b). Since 2001, however, negotiations have become the main tactic of choice for the Innu, but they have moved slowly, with little indication that a Final Agreement is ever forthcoming.

It is difficult to say with any certainty why the Innu adopted more confrontational strategies and why the Inuit for the most part avoided them. One answer might be that Inuit culture is very much consensus-driven and non-confrontational, only resorting to confrontation when there is no other choice. Geographer Robert McPherson has observed that "consensus building was the Inuit way" during Nunavut comprehensive land claims negotiations (McPherson, 2003: 140). Former Nisga'a federal negotiator Tom Molloy, quoted by McPherson, also noted that "unlike a great many Aboriginal peoples worldwide, the Inuit did not have to resort to litigation to have their rights acknowledged. That alone made the time and effort worthwhile" (ibid.: 270). My own interviews with federal, provincial, and Labrador Inuit officials indicated that in general the Labrador Inuit are perceived as preferring negotiated solutions to confrontation.

In terms of the Innu, the literature (see Alcantara, 2010; Backhouse and McRae, 2002; Samson, 2003) and interview data suggest that their propensity for confrontation probably stemmed from the effects of state interference in their lives. The provincial government has long engaged in disruptive actions on Innu lands. It has settled, under-serviced, and moved Innu communities throughout Labrador over the last fifty years. These actions have created Innu communities that are angry and in crisis, suffering from intense political, social, and economic problems. The natural response to such actions is to engage in occupations, protests, and blockades that express one's frustration in immediate and direct ways.

Some may suggest that the Labrador cases indicate that the use of confrontational tactics may be appropriate in some instances as tools for breaking a negotiating impasse or jumpstarting negotiations. Indeed, the use of protests and litigation by the Inuit and the Innu during the Voisey's Bay discovery helped to jumpstart their individual negotiations. However, only the Inuit were able to complete a treaty. Part of the reason for this difference in outcomes is that the Inuit used these types of tactics sparingly (once). By contrast, the Innu used them frequently over a long period of time to address a variety of issues, thus creating a significant impediment to treaty negotiations.

Aboriginal Group Cohesion as It Relates to Treaty Negotiations

Another factor affecting whether a CLC outcome is obtained is the cohesiveness of the Aboriginal community as it relates to the treaty process (see, for instance, Backhouse and McRae, 2002: 42, 50; Dewar, 2009: 76; Shafto, 2006; Serson, 2006; Warren, 2006; Whittington, 2005). In general, the Innu are a people beset with divisive leadership, internal division, and strife, much of which has been generated by the disruptive and as- similative actions of the federal and provincial governments over the last hundred years. These divisions have spilled over into the treaty process, making treaty negotiations difficult to pursue, let alone com- plete. According to a Sheshatshiu elder, "I think a lot of good things could come out from the agreement if only all the Innu worked coop- eratively, that is if Innu do not fight with each other. That is the biggest headache in this community today, because a lot of people hate each other. They just don't get along" (Innu Nation, 1998: 23). According to an Innu Nation community consultation report: "Some people com- plain that the Band Council and the Innu Nation only help some peo- ple, like their relatives, and not others. They don't see some people as their responsibility, even if they really need help ... They [Innu respon- dents] say our leaders are money-chasing and become blindfolded by the dollar sign" (Innu Nation, 1995: 171). For instance, according to the late Innu Nation president, Ben Michel, some members on the Innu Na- tion board of directors had demanded preferential access to the busi- ness contracts that would eventually come out of the Churchill Falls hydroelectric project and a final treaty settlement. Michel had opposed these directors, resulting in them organizing to push him out of office (CBC, 2006a; CBC, 2006c; Michel, 2006). These types of leadership con- flicts, both treaty-related and not, seem to be the norm in Innu Nation politics and in the politics of the Innu communities (see, for instance, CBC, 2004; CBC, 2006d).

   In addition to divisive leadership, the Innu suffer from severe social and economic problems, much of which is related to alcohol and sub- stance abuse (CBC, 2005c). In the words of a Davis Inlet elder, "There are too many suicides, too much gas sniffing and overdosing, too much vandalism, too many people in jail. Young people especially are ru- ined" (Innu Nation, 1998: 21). Between 1965 to February 1992, for exam- ple, 71 per cent of deaths in the community were alcohol-related; 49 per cent of those deaths involved people under the age of twenty, and 48 per cent were under the age of forty. From 1989 to February 1992 there were seventeen alcohol-related deaths. From February 1991 to February 1992 90 per cent of provincial court cases involving Innu were a result of alcohol abuse. Finally, in terms of children, there were forty cases of solvent abuse in 1990 and sixty-six cases in 1991 (Innu Nation, 1995: 187).

The point here is that domestic problems and internal conflicts have overtaken any sustained community interest or effort to negotiate a CLC agreement. Indeed, Innu leaders and community members have been divided since 1977 on whether they should negotiate a CLC agreement at all. Some leaders and community members, such as Daniel Ashini and Ben Michel, believe that negotiations are moving too fast and that there should be more of a focus on solutions to community problems. Others, like Peter Penashue and Paul Rich, see a CLC as a solution to these problems (CBC, 19 November 2006; Rich, 2006; Michel, 2006). The Innu communities have divided into these two factions, which has paralysed progress not only on land claims, but also efforts to address social and economic issues in the communities.

Contrast the Innu experience to that of the Inuit, who have not had political divisions and domestic problems interfere significantly with their treaty negotiations. Federal and provincial interviewees have identified the Inuit's clear and consistent leadership, strong capacity, and relatively few internal problems as key factors in their completed agreement. Community support and cohesion have also been strong. All the Inuit I interviewed mentioned that the communities have always supported negotiations throughout the entire process, reflecting a general Inuit trait of consensus-building rather than conflict. Inuit negotiators were able to come to the table with the knowledge that they had the support of the people. They were not distracted by severe community divisions or harsh economic and social problems. Having a cohesive community allowed the Inuit negotiators to negotiate in confidence and with their full attention and resources.[15] Community cohesion is also important because a negotiated agreement-in-principle and final agreement must be ratified by the entire population of each Aboriginal community, usually through a referendum. Without community cohesion and support for the negotiating team, ratification of any initialled agreements becomes impossible.

Cohesiveness, as is illustrated above and in the subsequent chapter, seems to be a crucial factor. It is crucial to the extent to which community divisions and problems bleed into the comprehensive land claims process. In the case of the Innu, its political, social, and economic problems have come to dominate the treaty process. In the case of the Inuit, the treaty process remained relatively immune and separate from the other problems affecting their society. Therefore, Aboriginal group cohesiveness matters only to the extent to which it directly affects and influences the modern treaty process.[16]

Government Perceptions

Another factor affecting whether a CLC outcome is obtained is government perceptions of the Aboriginal group. In general, government officials want to avoid international and domestic embarrassment when they complete treaties with Aboriginal peoples.[17] Government officials are aware of the negative publicity that can result if they devolve powers to a group that is not ready to take on the responsibilities of a land claims agreement. Government perceptions of the Aboriginal group determine the willingness of governments to devolve land management and self-government responsibilities to the Aboriginal group both on the long and short roads of negotiations. Perceptions are strongly influenced by the interactions between Aboriginal and government officials and agencies. Three government perceptions of Aboriginal groups matter: Aboriginal groups' capacity for financial accountability, their capacity for negotiations and self-government, and their degree of acculturation. If an Aboriginal group is perceived poorly on any of these indicators, it is unlikely that an agreement will get completed in either the long or the short term.

Governments are interested in negotiating agreements with those Aboriginal groups that have a demonstrated record of financial accountability and capacity for negotiations and self-government. The Inuit were able to demonstrate both of these attributes. LIA negotiators came to the table prepared for and skilled at negotiating with government officials according to the terms and the procedures of the comprehensive land claims process (Haysom, 2006; Marshall, 2006; Rowell, 2006; Shafto, 2006; Warren, 2006). LIA leaders and negotiators also brought to the table a record of financial accountability and capacity for governing themselves (Shafto, 2006; Andersen III, 2006; Barbour, 2006; Marshall, 2006; Mike Samson, 2006; Shafto, 2006). According to former LIA president William Barbour, government officials during a visit to Nain in the late 1990s remarked to him that the LIA "have the cleanest books in all of Atlantic Canada" (Barbour, 2006). This record of financial accountability is confirmed by the fact that they have never fallen under third-party management. Others have admired the LIA's administration of government services in Labrador Inuit communities. In the late 1980s, for instance, the LIA took control over post-secondary Inuit support programs from the province. Since 1987, the LIA-administered program has produced over five hundred graduates, compared to the seven or eight graduates produced when the province ran the program

(Andersen III, 2006; Tony Andersen, 2006; Barbour, 2006). In 1982 the LIA created the Labrador Inuit Alcohol and Drug Abuse Program, and in 1985 it secured federal funding to hire an interpreter/translator and set up a community health representative program. Moreover, in 1989, the LIA became one of only a few Aboriginal groups in Canada to take over the administration of the non-insured health benefits program for its communities (Baikie, 1990). Health Canada was so impressed with how the LIA administered this program that it informed the LIA that they were going to adopt some of the LIA practices and policies in the administration of their own non-insured health benefits program. Overall, the LIA demonstrated to the federal and provincial governments that they could deliver programs more effectively and at a lower cost to Inuit communities than the province or federal government could (Andersen III, 2006; Tony Andersen, 2006; Barbour, 2006).

Contrast these positive perceptions with the negative perceptions that the governments have of the Innu. A number of interviewees have characterized government perceptions of the Innu as paternalistic – father to child (Andrew, 2006; Michel, 2006). The media and the federal government have all observed the difficulties that the Innu have had in managing their fiscal affairs (Backhouse and McRae, 2002; CBC, 2006e; CBC, 2005b; Nui, 2006; Shafto, 2006). Premier Brian Peckford, at the First Ministers Constitutional Conference on Aboriginal Rights in March 1987, told Innu participants, "I'm not sure you're being as smart as you think you're being" (quoted in Wadden, 1991: 117). In a meeting with then minister of Indian affairs Pierre Cadieux, Peter Penashue remarked, "Could you get the mandate to treat us like adults? ... We have to find a way for the Canadian government to treat us like adults" (quoted ibid.: 166). According to Backhouse and McRae (2002),

It is not clear that the federal or provincial governments see self-government for the Innu in the foreseeable future. There is a strong sense among some officials that the Innu do not have the capacity to engage in self-government or to manage education or health services. Some [government officials] consider that a period of operating under the Indian Act will be a valuable "capacity-developing" experience for the Innu. Under this view, self-government is postponed even further into the future, perhaps indefinitely. (50)

Elsewhere, Backhouse and McRae (2002: 42) mention that some government officials believe that a land claim will cause more problems than it will solve. Other officials question the ability and capacity of the Innu to take on the responsibilities of land management under a CLC agreement.

Another government perception that seems to matter is the degree of acculturation of the Aboriginal community. In the context of CLC negotiations, the term refers to the level at which a group is familiar with Western institutions, processes, ideas, culture, and languages. The government's perception of a group's level of acculturation may be a factor in the willingness of a government to negotiate towards a settlement (Nadasdy 2003: 5). According to this argument, each Aboriginal group's familiarity with Canada's official languages and political processes affects how they are perceived by the participating governments and how successful they can be in navigating the CLC negotiation process.

In general, the Inuit are much more acculturated to Canadian society than the Innu, partly because they were influenced by the Moravian missionaries who settled among them several hundred years ago. A good example of Inuit acculturation is language. Most Inuit in Labrador have been educated in Western schools and now only speak English. According to 2001 census data for the five main Inuit communities on the coast of Labrador, English was the first learned and solely understood language among 81.1 per cent of the Inuit population, while 0.4 per cent spoke French and 18.5 per cent spoke Inuttut. Contrast this to the Innu: according to 2001 census data, only 13.2 per cent of Innu members speak English and 86.8 per cent speak Innuaimun, the Labrador Innu language, as their first languages. According to some government observers, the Innu face a real capacity problem, having few leaders who can successfully navigate Canadian institutions and negotiation processes. They also face a communication problem, as Innu leaders have at times found it difficult to explain the land claims process and land claims terminology such as "quantum" to community members. Many land claims concepts do not have an equivalent word in Innuaimun. Although the evidence is not as conclusive about the effect of acculturation on negotiations, several interviewees did mention that it did seem to play a role in the willingness of governments to negotiate a settlement.

It is hard to say whether acculturation is a problem of "perception" or a problem of "communication." It was extremely difficult to ask government officials whether acculturation affected their perceptions of the Aboriginal groups. Most chose not to answer the question, or they chose to give the obvious answer – of course acculturation does not matter. The literature, however, argues that it does matter. Paul Nadasdy (2003), for instance, argues that the level of acculturation determines whether governments will take Aboriginal group seriously at the negotiating table. Although the evidence regarding this assertion for the Labrador land claims is not conclusive, a number of interviewees indicated it may have had a role in shaping government perceptions.

An Update on the Innu Negotiations

So far, much of the evidence in this chapter suggests that the Innu are highly unlikely to complete a modern treaty any time in the near future. However, some recent developments have generated modest optimism. Since 2001, the Innu have abandoned protest tactics in favour of cooperating with the federal and provincial governments. They have also generated positive government perceptions by becoming Indian bands under the Indian Act and by focusing on land claims negotiations and on a Lower Churchill impact and benefits agreement. There is also some evidence that compatible goals may be possible. The death of Ben Michel and the election of Peter Penashue, who was president of Innu Nation when the Innu signed their land claims framework agreement in 1996, have resulted in a set of leaders willing to work within the processes and goals of the federal and provincial governments. Finally, to avoid community-level delays, Penashue has reduced the number of community consultations, which, as will be discussed in the next chapter, helped the KDFN in the Yukon to successfully complete their negotiations with the federal and territorial governments.

Despite these positive developments, as of September 2009, a number of deadlines relating to further agreements and a community ratification vote related to the New Dawn Agreement have passed without any significant progress being made. Nonetheless, community leaders continue to negotiate with the Crown in hopes of completing the agreements associated with the New Dawn Agreement and to eventually hold a ratification vote.

Factors Affecting Speed

The four factors discussed above are what ultimately determined the final outcomes of the Inuit and Innu negotiations. Table 2.2 below lists the factors that affected the speed and pace of both negotiations.

Table 2.2 Factors that affect the speed of CLC negotiation outcomes

Factors affecting quickly completed treaties	Factors affecting prolonged completed treaties
– Presence of trust relationships between governments and Aboriginal groups – Presence of supportive governmental negotiators and presence of an external government negotiator – Low competition for use of Aboriginal-claimed lands – High development pressure affecting Aboriginal-claimed lands	– Lack of trust relationships between governments and Aboriginal groups – Lack of supportive governmental negotiators and lack of an external government negotiator – High competition for use of Aboriginal claimed-lands – Low development pressure affecting Aboriginal-claimed lands

Trust Relationships

One important factor that can affect the pace of negotiations is the ability of Aboriginal negotiators and officials to develop professional trust relationships with their federal and provincial counterparts (see Dewar, 2009: 76; Fenge and Quassa, 2009: 83). According to all the negotiators, the trust built between negotiators post-1996 was an important factor for completing the Inuit agreement (Mackenzie, 2006; Serson, 2006; Warren, 2006; Pain, 2006; Haysom, 2006). Trust allowed the negotiators to propose ideas to each other outside of the formal negotiating process without fear that these proposals would be used against them in future formal negotiation sessions. The negotiators knew that their proposals and counter-proposals were sincere and that each side would be willing to make an effort to be as clear as possible about their negotiating mandates and their flexibility regarding those mandates. There was also trust between Inuit leaders and federal and provincial executives at critical junctures. The success of the October 1997 meetings, for instance, was partly due to the strong relationships between Scott Serson, deputy minister of INAC, Chesley Andersen of the LIA, and Harold Marshall from Newfoundland and Labrador. In another instance, one negotiator mentioned the importance of an informal agreement between the LIA president, premier, and federal minister to complete the Final Agreement as quickly as possible if Inco suddenly became ready to begin mining in Voisey's Bay before the Inuit treaty was finished. Relationships between Innu negotiators and their counterparts, by contrast, have not been as productive. According to government sources, some Innu negotiators have been confrontational and combative, with highly unreasonable expectations and demands.

Trust relationships affect the speed of negotiations as opposed to whether an outcome is obtained. If the Inuit had not built trust relationships with the federal and provincial governments, other factors would have resulted in a completed treaty. This outcome would have occurred because government negotiators must report to senior civil servants and elected politicians, who, on the basis of compatible goals, the Aboriginal group's choice of strategies, the Aboriginal group's internal cohesiveness, and government perceptions of the Aboriginal group, can direct their negotiators to complete a deal (although without trust relationships, such negotiations might take longer to complete). Or, senior officials can decide to simply replace the government negotiators. Moreover, as will be shown in the next chapter, the Kaska First Nations were unable to complete their treaties despite forging trust relationships with government negotiators. Instead, the Kaska had incompatible goals, weak internal cohesion, and poor government perceptions, and frequently used litigation, resulting in unsuccessful treaty negotiations despite strong trust relationships between the Kaska's chief negotiator, Dave Porter, and his federal and territorial counterparts. Therefore, trust relationships do not determine whether an outcome is obtained; rather, they are important for affecting the pace of negotiations. The presence of trust can speed up negotiations, whereas its absence can make progress more difficult.

Government and External Negotiators

Government negotiators can matter in two specific ways. First, a non-bureaucrat negotiator is important because she is usually not subject to the same hierarchical constraints as a bureaucratic negotiator (Haysom, 2006; Pain, 2006; Rowell, 2006; Warren, 2006; Whittington, 2005). In the fall of 1996, the federal government appointed Jim Mackenzie, a non-bureaucrat and law professor from Carleton University, as chief federal negotiator to sit beside the senior federal negotiator (a bureaucrat) at the Inuit table. Mackenzie was effective because he initially had direct access to the minister of Indian affairs and was not subject to the hierarchy that bureaucratic negotiators tend to face. Contrast this with the previous bureaucrat negotiator, during whose tenure little progress was made, partly because she was trapped within the bureaucratic lines of authority. She constantly had to clear negotiation items with her superiors, which frequently delayed negotiations and annoyed Aboriginal negotiators. Although it is true that in theory a bureaucrat negotiator could enjoy the same leeway and access that a non-bureaucrat negotiator has, usually this does not happen. Rather, the minister usually replaces a bureaucrat negotiator with an external negotiator to speed up a set of negotiations that have been moving too slowly for the minister's liking.

The federal government did appoint an external chief federal negotiator for the Innu in the late 1990s. However, this negotiator has focused on other issues such as registration and reserve creation, policing, justice, and healing services. So far, he has had little to do with the land claims negotiations, meaning that the Innu continue to deal solely with bureaucrat negotiators (Innes, 2006; Riche, 2006).

Second, the commitment and personality of the negotiator seems to matter. Provincial and LIA interviewees agreed that the provincial negotiator, Bob Warren, was extremely important in getting a deal done. Although Warren was a provincial bureaucrat, it was clear he believed in the LIA and was willing to "go the extra mile" within the provincial bureaucracy to get the deal. According to one anonymous observer, Warren was at one point seen by his colleagues in the provincial bureaucracy as being more committed to the Inuit than the province. Yet Warren had both the necessary expertise and the respect within the provincial bureaucracy to work effectively on behalf of Inuit concerns. This is not to say that Warren was not tough or mindful of provincial concerns at the negotiating table. However, it was clear that his commitment to the Inuit, and his expertise, energy, and the respect he commanded in the bureaucracy were invaluable in moving Inuit negotiations forward during the critical period from the framework agreement to the AIP. The case of Warren suggests that government negotiators can sometimes be an impediment to the timely completion of a final agreement.

These two factors affect speed as opposed to whether an outcome is obtained because government negotiators, whether they are bureaucrats or third-party negotiators, are subject to higher political authorities. If the deputy minister, minister, premier, or prime minister are not interested in a deal, then it does not matter if an external negotiator is present or if a provincial negotiator is committed to a deal. Moreover, an agreement could be reached without the presence of an external negotiator or a provincial negotiator who believed in the Aboriginal group. For instance, the October 1997 Inuit meeting in Ottawa would have taken place and resolved the critical issues delaying Inuit negotiations even if there were no third-party negotiator or pro-Inuit provincial negotiator present.

Competition for Use of Claimed Lands and Development Pressure

In terms of development pressure, during the 1970s and 1980s, the federal and provincial governments issued property rights to third parties to develop those Aboriginal lands (mostly Innu in Labrador) that they knew or speculated had significant economic value. These property rights were important because third-party interests (lands in which non-government groups have licences and other interests) are excluded from land claims negotiations unless the parties agree to freeze such lands from development. As a result, the governments were in no hurry to complete treaty negotiations with the Innu and the Inuit since they could immediately benefit from the exploitation of Labrador's valuable lands without treaties.

Things changed, however, with the discovery of nickel at Voisey's Bay. Negotiations for both the Innu and the Inuit accelerated after the discovery because the area was not subject to third-party interests. The result was the rapid negotiation and completion of the Innu's and the Inuit's Voisey's Bay chapters and impact and benefit agreements, which cleared the way for development. Yet only the Inuit were able to complete a CLC treaty, mainly because they had compatible goals, rarely used confrontational tactics, had strong internal cohesion, and generated positive government perceptions. Conversely, the Innu did not complete a treaty because they had incompatible goals, a history of confrontational tactics, weak internal cohesion, and negative government perceptions. Indeed, despite the provincial government's interest in the latest large-scale economic development opportunity in Labrador, the Lower Churchill hydroelectric project, land claims negotiations seem to have little chance of completion any time in the near future. The land quantum in the 2008 New Dawn Agreement is far smaller than what community members seem to want. As well, the New Dawn Agreement does not deal with the issue of certainty and finality, which is at the core of the Innu's reluctance to complete a treaty. The New Dawn Agreement, however, does commit the parties to resolve this issue in a subsequent agreement, which may be possible in light of the death of Ben Michel and the election of pro-land claims leader Peter Penashue as grand chief of the Innu.

In terms of the effect of competition for land use, Michael Whittington, chief federal negotiator in the Yukon from 1987 to 1993, has argued that "the more remote FNs [in the Yukon] settled earlier because their land selections were less constrained by competing uses" (Whittington, 2005). This dynamic was also in play for the Labrador groups. The Inuit claim involved mostly remote and homogeneous regions in the province where the Inuit were by far the majority. As a result, the provincial and federal governments had fewer third parties to accommodate in the final agreement. The Innu claim, by contrast, involves land in central and southern Labrador where they are the minority, meaning that the federal and provincial governments are subject to substantial third-party pressure. Since the Innu are a minority and any agreement will have an impact on the lives of the majority in the area, crafting a deal that satisfies the non-Aboriginal majority is important for both governments (Pelley, 2006; Warren, 2006).

Conclusion

This chapter has argued that four factors explain variation in treaty negotiation outcomes for the Inuit and the Innu in Labrador. These factors are compatibility of goals, choice of tactics, Aboriginal group cohesion as it relates to treaty negotiations, and government perceptions of the Aboriginal group. The ability of Aboriginal groups to influence these factors is partially affected by a number of conditioning influences, such as the nature of Indigenous acculturation and historical interactions with the Canadian state (e.g., the forced resettlement of the Innu). Other factors such as trust relationships, the attributes of individual government and external negotiators, competition for the use of claimed lands, and the emergence of development pressures can accelerate negotiations, but these factors have little effect on whether negotiations will in fact be completed.

Although the four factors described above that explain variation in treaty negotiation outcomes are not directly taken from the theoretical literature surveyed in the first part of this book, they flow logically from that analytical framework. Aboriginal groups and government actors operate within an institutional framework that privileges government interests over Aboriginal ones. As well, Aboriginal and non-Aboriginal interests diverge to the extent that Aboriginal groups in the treaty process tend to see a final agreement as pareto-superior to no treaty, whereas the opposite is true for the Crown. As a result, treaty completion will depend on the ability of the Aboriginal groups to convince the Crown that a treaty is in its best interests. The four factors described above are crucial to this task.

Chapter Three

The Kwanlin Dün First Nation and the Kaska Nations in the Yukon Territory

In contrast to other Aboriginal groups in Canada, the fourteen First Nations in the Yukon Territory[1] decided to negotiate an Umbrella Final Agreement (UFA) with the federal and Yukon governments. Once the UFA was completed, each Yukon First Nation was to use it as a template for negotiating individual final agreements. Although each First Nation could negotiate specific provisions that gave the template provisions greater relevance to particular circumstances and interests, many things were unchangeable, including the number and type of powers, lands, and jurisdictions.

Throughout the Yukon process, government and Aboriginal policymakers were optimistic about completing the Yukon treaties. For instance, the Yukon First Nations were one of the original six groups that the federal government initiated negotiations with in the mid-1970s, believing that it could complete the Yukon treaties relatively quickly. In 1993 the negotiating parties achieved an Umbrella Final Agreement and individual final agreements with four Yukon First Nations. Although seven additional Yukon First Nations completed individual treaties after the original four, three, the White River First Nation and the Kaska nations of Liard and Ross River, have not.

So what explains these divergent outcomes? Why did the Yukon processes fail to produce completed treaties for all fourteen nations, despite relatively strong optimism? To answer these questions, this chapter examines the experiences of the Kwanlin Dün First Nation (completed) and the Kaska nations of Ross River Dena Council and Liard First Nation (incomplete). Although most of the factors from the previous chapter were at play in the Yukon cases, the Yukon cases emphasize the importance of Aboriginal group cohesion and Aboriginal leadership for explaining divergent outcomes.

Who Are the Kwanlin Dün and the Kaska?

Maps

Two maps presented here are relevant to the contents of this chapter. Map 3.1 illustrates the main cities, highways, and waterways of the Yukon Territory. Map 3.2 shows the traditional territories of the Kwanlin Dün First Nation (KDFN) and the Kaska Nation.

A Brief History of the Kwanlin Dün

Anthropologists (LegendSeekers Anthropological Research, 2000; Catherine McClellan, 1981) have classified Kwanlin Dün members as belonging to the broad Athapaskan language category and the Southern Tutchone cultural and linguistic sub-category. Its traditional territories are made up of the lands along the Yukon River from Lake Laberge to Marsh Lake and downriver to Hootalinqua. At the heart of its traditional territories are the lands in the city of Whitehorse and along the Yukon River. Its most important traditional lands are those alongside the Yukon River in Whitehorse. It is here that Kwanlin Dün members historically spent much of their time living in seasonal fish camps to harvest salmon (Kwanlin Dün First Nation, 2003). When not living along the Yukon River, members hunted and fished along the shores of the other lakes in their traditional territories, such as at Fish Lake, Bonneville Lakes, Marsh Lake (Kwanlin Dün First Nation, 1994: 11), and Lake Laberge (Kwanlin Dün First Nation, 2003: 2; INAC, 2005). Kwanlin Dün members were not alone in travelling and using their traditional territories. In addition to welcoming visiting Aboriginal peoples from other Yukon First Nations (Kwanlin Dün First Nation, 2003: 3), they also shared significant parts of their territories with the ancestors of the Ta'an Kwäch'än First Nation. Ta'an members tended to spend most of their time in the northern part of Kwanlin Dün's territories, especially in the area around Lake Laberge. Members of the Kwanlin Dün and Ta'an Kwäch'än interacted with each other relatively freely, trading, travelling, and sometimes working together to hunt and fish.

First contact with the settler society occurred probably in 1842, when Robert Campbell came to the Yukon on behalf of the Hudson's Bay

Map 3.1

Company. In 1848 he founded Fort Selkirk at the mouth of the Pelly River. This settlement was a trading post for Northern and Southern Tutchone peoples to acquire European goods until 1852, when the Coastal Tlingit peoples drove Campbell and his followers out of Fort Selkirk. The next major European-Canadian settlement to emerge in the Yukon was in 1874 at Fort Reliance, just south of what is now known as Dawson City. In the 1880s and the 1890s, a number of European-Canadian and European-American explorers came to the Yukon Territory searching for mineral resources and trading routes (McClellan, 1981: 493, 503).

The life of Kwanlin Dün members underwent dramatic change as a result of the gold rush in the late 1890s and the creation of the city of Whitehorse in the early 1900s. The gold rush brought large numbers of non-Aboriginal peoples to the Yukon Territory and through Kwanlin Dün lands. In addition to bringing trade and disease, the large influx of prospectors reduced the amount of wildlife in the area, pushing Kwanlin Dün members ten to twenty miles further inland to find game

Map 3.2

(Kwanlin Dün First Nation, 2003: 6). As non-Aboriginal prospectors arrived to claim tracts of land, all Aboriginal peoples, including Kwanlin Dün members, were excluded from making claims to mining areas. Instead, they were hired as hunting guides or as low-wage labourers in mining camps (Coates, 1991).

In the early 1900s, the White Pass and Yukon Railway Company purchased and sold the land that was to become the downtown core of the city of Whitehorse. Kwanlin Dün members, who had previously spent most of their time along various parts of the Yukon River, were moved to the east bank, north of the current Whitehorse General Hospital site. In 1912 Kwanlin Dün members were again moved, but this time to the west side of the Yukon River (now known as the Robert Service Campground). As the city grew, so did the Aboriginal population as Aboriginal peoples flocked to Whitehorse to take advantage of the opportunities available in the city. In 1915, Indian superintendent John Hawsley asked the Department of Indian Affairs to set aside land for Kwanlin Dün members. The department did this in 1921, creating Lot 226, "the Old Village," for Kwanlin Dün and Ta'an members to live on (INAC, 2005; Kwanlin Dün First Nation, 2003: 6–7).

In the early 1940s the American government began construction of the Alaska Highway, resulting in another influx of non-Aboriginal peoples to the Yukon Territory. As a result, Whitehorse's population expanded rapidly. Aboriginal peoples took advantage of this influx to again act as hunting guides, work as low-wage labourers, and sell their traditional crafts. In 1953 the government of the Yukon Territory declared Whitehorse to be the territorial capital. In 1956 the Department of Indian Affairs amalgamated Kwanlin Dün and Ta'an Kwäch'än members to form the Whitehorse Indian Band (Kwanlin Dün First Nation, 2003: 7–8). In addition to Kwanlin Dün and Ta'an Kwäch'än members, all other First Nations members living in Whitehorse became band members of the Whitehorse Indian Band. Government officials referred to these non-Kwanlin Dün and Ta'an Kwäch'än members as "come from aways" (Armour, 2006; Flynn, 2006; King, 2006; Koepke, 2006). The idea behind the creation of the Whitehorse Indian Band was to make it easier for the Department of Indian Affairs to administer programs and services to all Aboriginal peoples living in Whitehorse. This decision to amalgamate all Aboriginal peoples living in Whitehorse into one First Nation, however, would complicate the ability of the KDFN to complete a modern treaty.

In 1962 the federal and territorial governments removed all remaining Whitehorse Indian band members from their riverfront lands in Whitehorse, except for those members living on Lot 226, the Old Village. After the *Calder* decision in 1973, a delegation of Yukon First Nations leaders travelled to Ottawa to initiate the comprehensive land claims process for Yukon First Nations. In 1984 the Whitehorse Indian Band changed its name to Kwanlin Dün First Nation. Around the same time, the government built the McIntyre subdivision to house workers for the construction of the proposed Alaska Highway pipeline project. However, this project never went ahead and in 1985 the government offered the McIntyre subdivision to the Kwanlin Dün. Kwanlin Dün's chief and council agreed to the offer, and most band members moved from Lot 226 to the McIntyre subdivision. Today, the majority of Kwanlin Dün's members live in this subdivision, about a ten-minute drive from the banks of the Yukon River.

In 1993 the Kwanlin Dün and the Ta'an Kwäch'än communities signed the UFA as separate signatories, and in 1998 INAC minister Jane Stewart formally separated them into two First Nations. In 2002 the Ta'an Kwäch'än completed its treaty, and in February 2005 the Kwanlin Dün negotiators completed theirs. As of 1 April 2005, the Kwanlin Dün First Nation has been governing itself and administering its lands according to the terms of its treaty agreements.

According to data provided by Indian and Northern Affairs Canada (Gour, 2006), Kwanlin Dün First Nation had 951 registered members in 2001, 957 members in 2003, and 959 members in 2005. In February 2007, INAC (2007) reported that Kwanlin Dün First Nation had 951 registered members. What is unclear from these data is how many registered members are beneficiaries (traditional Kwanlin Dün "citizens") and how many are non-beneficiaries (citizens from other First Nations). The Kwanlin Dün First Nation has identified 634 beneficiaries (Kwanlin Dün First Nation, 2005: 3), but neither it nor INAC have stated how many of these beneficiaries are band members and how many are non-band members. The best educated guess is extrapolated from the Kwanlin Dün Final Agreement ratification results in 2005. According to those results, 66.3 per cent of Kwanlin Dün eligible voters were beneficiaries and band members, 9.2 per cent were beneficiaries but not band members, while 24.5 per cent were members but not beneficiaries. INAC (2005) reports that approximately half of Kwanlin Dün beneficiaries live in Whitehorse.

A Brief History of the Kaska

Anthropologists (LegendSeekers Anthropological Research, 2000; Honigmann, 1964) have classified the Kaska as a distinct cultural and linguistic group within the broad Athapaskan language category. The Kaska's traditional lands are in the southeastern part of the Yukon Territory and in northern British Columbia. Although the Kaska used to have numerous settlements throughout their traditional lands, today most Kaska members in the Yukon Territory live in Ross River, Upper Liard, and Watson Lake. Upper Liard and Watson Lake are governed by Liard First Nation, whereas Ross River and its surrounding areas are controlled by Ross River Dena Council. Kaska leaders in the Yukon Territory and in British Columbia collectively claim as their traditional lands approximately 25 per cent of the southeastern part of the Yukon Territory, and 10 per cent of BC Kaska lands in the Yukon are some of the richest in the territory in terms of forests, minerals, and fish and wildlife resources.

Pre-contact, most Kaska groups and individuals relied heavily on hunting and trading with other Aboriginal groups as their main sources of income. After contact, many Kaska groups and individuals took up the fur trade to make their living, frequently travelling to the Hudson's Bay Company's posts in Upper Liard (near Watson Lake, YT), Fort Frances (near Ross River, YT), and Lower Post (in northern British Columbia) to trade their furs for European goods (Honigmann, 1981: 443).

The first sustained contact with non-Aboriginal peoples probably occurred in the 1820s when the Hudson's Bay Company opened a trading post at Fort Halkett on the Liard River in northern British Columbia. In 1843 the Hudson's Bay Company opened another trading post on Kaska lands, right on the shores of Frances Lake, near present-day Ross River. This post was closed by the Hudson's Bay Company in 1852, only to be reopened in 1880. In addition to traders, European trappers came to the area in search of fur. In 1873 small groups of non-Aboriginal prospectors came looking for gold in Kaska lands, and then in 1898, large groups of prospectors came through Kaska lands on their way to the Klondike gold fields (Honigmann, 1981: 442; Coates, 1991).

Once the gold rush ended, many of the non-Aboriginal prospectors left the Yukon. In their place were Protestant and Catholic missionaries, who set up temporary missions to serve the Kaska peoples. In 1926 Father Allard of the Catholic church opened a permanent mission on the banks of the Dease River to educate and convert Kaska peoples. Sustained contact with the settler society came in 1942, when the US government began construction of the Alaska Highway. This highway was built alongside the Kaska communities of Lower Post, BC, and Upper Liard in the Yukon Territory (Coates, 1991; McClellan, 1987). The proximity of the highway to these Kaska communities increased the frequency of sexual contact between Kaska women and non-Aboriginal men, as well as introducing alcohol to these Kaska communities (Honigmann, 1981: 442–3). It also facilitated the construction of the Canadian community of Watson Lake, just outside of Upper Liard. Once the highway was completed, many Kaska members used it and its subsidiary roads to travel about their lands to hunt, fish, and trade with their Aboriginal and non-Aboriginal neighbours. In 1966 the Canadian government helped the Cyprus Anvil Mining Corporation to open a mine approximately 67 kilometres west of the Kaska village of Ross River. Although the mine generated substantial revenues for the Crown, it

had a profoundly negative impact on the Kaska. In addition to inter-
fering with the Kaska's use of their lands in its environs, the mine employed very few Kaska. Moreover, the opening of the mine led to the
founding of the town of Faro, where the miners lived. The proximity
of Faro to Ross River ensured that alcohol was easily introduced and
readily available to Kaska members in Ross River. Today, alcoholism
remains a major problem among Kaska members in Ross River (Barichello, 2006; Koepke, 2006; Sterriah, 2006; Van Bibber, 2006) and has
weakened the Aboriginal group's cohesiveness as it relates to treaty
negotiations.

In 1973 the Kaska nations of Ross River Dena Council and Liard First
Nation joined together with the other Yukon First Nations to begin comprehensive land claims negotiations with the federal government. In the
mid- to late 1980s, the Kaska communities decided to strengthen their
ties with each other by recognizing the existence of "one Kaska Nation."
In 1991 the Kaska created the Kaska Tribal Council (KTC) to coordinate
their activities as one Kaska Nation. Specifically, KTC was to act on their
behalf to negotiate one comprehensive land claims agreement for all
Kaska. However, the federal government refused to recognize the Kaska
Nation at the negotiating table until 1998. As of February 2008, Kaska negotiations in the Yukon are suspended as a result of the federal mandate
that expired in June 2002 (further details are provided below).

KTC, which is headquartered in Watson Lake, is governed by a democratically elected board of directors and a tribal chief. The only tribal
chief that KTC has ever had is Hammond Dick and the KTC's chief
negotiator has always been Dave Porter. Although KTC does provide
some minor program and monetary support to the Kaska band councils, the main purpose of KTC is to facilitate and coordinate Kaska comprehensive land claims negotiations in the Yukon Territory (Dick, 2006;
McMillan, 2006; Dave Porter, 2006).

Much like other First Nations in Canada, the Kaska communities in
the Yukon are governed by Indian Act band councils. Ross River Dena
Council is governed by one chief, one deputy chief, and three councillors. Liard First Nation is led by one chief, four councillors, and one
non-voting hereditary chief. Both band councils administer a number
of programs, including community infrastructure, capital projects, education, social assistance, social support, economic development, and
housing (Pike, 2006; McIntyre, 2006).

According to data provided by Indian and Northern Affairs Canada
(Gour, 2006), Liard First Nation had 983 registered members in 2001,

1005 members in 2003, and 1032 members in 2005. Ross River Dena Council had 419 members in 2001, 432 members in 2003, and 459 members in 2005. In February 2007 (INAC, 2007), Liard First Nation had 1057 members and Ross River Dena Council had 468 members. Although Kaska members are the clear majority in Ross River, a significant number of non-Aboriginal peoples live in and around Liard First Nation in Watson Lake.

The Yukon First Nations Experience: A Collective Approach to Comprehensive Land Claims Negotiations

In contrast to other regions in Canada, almost all Aboriginal peoples in the Yukon Territory never signed historical treaties with the Crown[2] nor did they ever receive reserve lands. After the *Calder* decision in 1973, the Yukon First Nations were one of the first Aboriginal groups in Canada to begin comprehensive land claims negotiations with the federal government. The federal government was highly motivated to negotiate with the Yukon First Nations for two main reasons. First, throughout the 1970s, the federal government was very interested in developing the rich, largely untapped resources of the Canadian North; settling the Yukon claims was an important first step for developing the Yukon Territory. Second, the Yukon First Nations showed significant promise in terms of their likelihood of completing an agreement quickly and in accordance with the preferences of the federal government. The government thought it could quickly complete a deal with the Yukon First Nations, which in turn would allow it to focus its attention on other more difficult claims (Joe, 2006; Mitander, 2006).

The Yukon First Nations' statement of intent, *Together Today for Our Children Tomorrow*, submitted to the federal government in 1973, signalled the group's desire to complete a treaty quickly. In that document, Yukon First Nations leaders described how their peoples became impoverished after the arrival of non-Aboriginal peoples in their lands (Yukon Indian Brotherhood, 1973: 7–13). As a result, they wanted to negotiate a treaty settlement that lifted their peoples out of this poverty (ibid.: 15–25). In particular, a treaty had to give the Yukon Indians the necessary tools to survive and prosper as Aboriginal peoples within modern Canadian society. According to part 4 of the document, a settlement would "help us and our children learn to live in a changing world. We want to take part in the development of the Yukon and Canada, not stop it. But we can only participate as Indians. We will not sell our heritage for a quick buck or a temporary job" (29). Moreover, "we have been accused of opposing the development of the North. If you are able to understand this final section of our paper, you will learn that we are strong supporters of development" as long as "'we' could control the direction and pace of that development" (48). In addition to Aboriginal control over development, a settlement had to lead to the creation of programs specifically for Indian peoples; it had to support Yukon Indian elders, recognize and protect Indian cultures and identities, and foster community development, education, economic development, and media, and allow for Indian-focused research (ibid.: part 4). The document ends by arguing that Yukon Indians preferred to negotiate a treaty as quickly as possible to avoid the costly delays that can arise from other settlement strategies. "We are asking that you agree with us on a quick Settlement to avoid a long fight in the Courts and in Parliament" (ibid.: 73).

Together Today for Our Children Tomorrow was a clear signal to the federal government that a "good" deal was possible with the Yukon Indians. The fact that the Yukon Indian leaders had filed a joint statement of intent indicated that they might be willing to adopt a collective approach to negotiating their comprehensive land claims. The Yukon Indian leaders also seemed to be pro-development and wanted to enter into negotiations rather than seek potentially more expensive and damaging actions through Canadian courts and Parliament (Mitander, 2006; Joe, 2006; McArthur, 2006; Nadasdy, 2003: 55; Penikett, 2006 [interview]). As such, federal officials saw the Yukon Indians as ideal candidates for active negotiations.

The Yukon Indians were represented at the negotiating table by the Yukon Native Brotherhood (representing status Indians in the Yukon) and the Yukon Association of Non-Status Indians (DIAND, 2002; Huggard, August 1987; McClellan, 1987: 99–104). In late 1973 the federal government initiated negotiations by making "a unilateral, public offer of settlement" to the two organizations (Frideres, 1986: 289). Both groups quickly rejected the offer, forcing the federal government to change its offer into a working offer open for negotiations. Formal negotiations began in early 1974 between the Yukon Native Brotherhood (YNB), the Yukon Association of Non-Status Indians (YANSI), and the federal government. At this point, the Yukon territorial government (YTG) did not have its own seat at the negotiating table. Rather, negotiations were bilateral and YTG officials sat as part of the federal negotiating team. To signal its displeasure with this situation, YTG published *Meaningful*

Government for All Yukoners. It was a blueprint for transforming the Yukon Territory into a province. Among other things, this document stressed the need for a "one-government system" (a provincial government) rather than a two-government system (a non-Aboriginal government co-existing with a Yukon Indian government) in the Yukon (Frideres, 1986: 289–90). The political and constitutional evolution of the Yukon Territory would transform the Yukon territorial government from passive participant to an equal and crucial negotiating partner. Its growing influence would later become important during the negotiation of issues that usually fall within the domain of provinces, such as land selection and resource regulation.

In 1975 the YNB, the YANSI, and the federal government agreed to "freeze" 12,000 square miles of Yukon land until a land claims agreement could be reached. Comprehensive land claims negotiations continued through to 1979, stopping briefly in 1977 and 1978 because of Yukon Indian opposition to the YTG's "one-government" policy. In 1979 the federal government invited YTG to join the negotiating table as a separate and equal negotiating party, much to the dismay of Yukon Indian leaders. At the same time, however, the parties agreed to "develop a Yukon constitutional development process to be correlated with the native claims process" (Frideres, 1986: 294). All four negotiating parties realized that land claims negotiations were very much tied to the political evolution of the territory.

In February 1980 the Yukon Native Brotherhood and the Yukon Association of Non-Status Indians decided to merge to form the Council for Yukon Indians (CYI), which would represent all Yukon Aboriginal peoples at the negotiating table (McClellan, 1987: 103). With the territorial government at the table and the Yukon Indian organizations amalgamated into one umbrella organization, comprehensive land claims negotiations moved forward relatively quickly. Later that same year, negotiators Dave Joe (CYI), Dennis O'Connor (DIAND), and Willard Phelps (YTG) reached an agreement on the issues of eligibility, wildlife use and management, and land use planning. In 1981 the negotiators came to an agreement on provisions relating to education, social programs, heath, harvesting, hunting, and fishing. At the same time, the Carcross, Pelly, Teslin, Champagne/Aishihik, and Burwash First Nations completed their land selections, thus creating optimism among the negotiators and the public that an agreement-in-principle was close at hand (Council for Yukon First Nations, n.d.; DIAND, 2002; Huggard, 1987; Joe, 2006; Mitander, 2006). In December 1982 the territorial government withdrew from the negotiating table due to a dispute with the federal government over the issues of costs, non-native land use, non-resident claimants, and the possible negative effects of a land claims agreement on the constitutional development of the territory. Nonetheless, negotiations between the CYI and the federal government continued, with significant progress being made. In light of this progress, the YTG returned to the table in April 1983. In that year, the three parties reached an agreement on boundary definitions, training, beneficiary programs, financial compensation, and corporate structures (Huggard, 1987; Joe, 2006; Mitander, 2006).

In early 1984 the four parties completed negotiations and signed an agreement-in principle (AIP), the main provisions of which were:

- 20,000 square kilometres to be distributed among all Yukon First Nations; out of that Old Crow First Nation would receive 7500 square kilometres because their lands were located in the most isolated areas of the Yukon.
- $130 million in financial compensation over twenty years.
- $53.69 million over twenty years in exchange for giving up access to federal programs for status Indians.
- special programs and powers for housing, education, health care, social services, and the administration of justice.
- Yukon Indians agreed to extinguish their Aboriginal title to all lands in Canada (Frideres, 1986: 296–8).

For the AIP to come into effect, the federal government decided that it needed to be ratified by at least nine of the twelve Yukon First Nations before the end of the year. In December 1984, at its general assembly in Tagish, the CYI failed to reach this threshold; specifically, the Mayo, the Carcross, and the two Kaska First Nations (Ross River Dena Council and Liard First Nation) voted against ratification. Their main issues of concern were extinguishment, self-government, equality rights between status and non-status Indians, and the amount of land to be transferred (Council for Yukon First Nations, n.d.; Joe, 2006; Koepke, 2006). Some First Nations, especially the Kaska First Nations, were concerned that the negotiations were conducted far too secretly. Negotiations at this stage were very much conducted in the classical "executive federalism" style, with little public input and transparency (Dick, 2006; Koepke, 2006; Mitander, 2006; Dave Porter, 2006; Raider, 2006; Van Bibber, 2006).

As a result of the CYI failing to ratify the AIP, the federal government immediately suspended formal negotiations and cut its funding to the CYI. One reason for the latter decision was that, in its view, negotiations had finished as a result of the CYI's failure to ratify the AIP, so there was no need to continue providing funds to the CYI. A second reason for the federal government's decision was that it was beginning a process to reform its comprehensive land claims policy (Abele, 1986: 170). Nonetheless, informal negotiations continued over how to restart negotiations. In November 1985 the three parties signed a memorandum of understanding (MOU) to restart negotiations. The MOU set out a new negotiating process for ensuring that the next AIP would be successfully ratified. In January 1986 the federal government restored funding to the CYI, and in March 1986 the Coolican report[3] was released. In December 1986 the federal government responded to the report by redesigning its comprehensive land claims policy. The key change to its policy was the deletion of the word "extinguishment" (ibid.: 171). At the same time that these events were occurring, the Kaska nations began to file the first of a dozen lawsuits, over a twenty-year period, against the federal government over the government's failure to abide by its fiduciary duty to resolve Kaska land claims (Huggard, 1987; Council for Yukon First Nations, n.d.; Joe, 2006; Mitander, 2006; Walsh, 2006).

In June 1987 the federal government, the YTG, and the CYI resumed land claims negotiations under the new federal comprehensive land claims policy. The negotiators made swift progress because the new federal policy gave the negotiating parties sufficient flexibility to address the problems that had led to the defeat of the 1984 AIP (Joe, 2006; Mitander, 2006; Koepke, 2006). In 1989 the three parties signed a new agreement-in-principle. Among other things, the new AIP increased the land quantum to 41,595.21 square kilometres, raised the financial compensation to $242.6 million, and called for the "cede, release, and surrender," but not the extinguishment, of Aboriginal title. With a completed AIP in place, negotiations turned to drafting an Umbrella Final Agreement. Again, negotiations proceeded quickly, and in early 1993 the CYI, the federal government, and the YTG completed and signed the Umbrella Final Agreement, which transformed the AIP into a final treaty. This time around, the federal government decided to allow the CYI to determine its own ratification process. In March 1993, at its usual quarterly board meeting, the CYI ratified the Umbrella Final Agreement despite the vigorous opposition of the Kaska nations. There was never any formal ratification vote held among all the Yukon Indians

(Dick, 2006; Joe, 2006; Mitander, 2006; Dave Porter, 2006; Raider, 2006; Sterriah, 2006; Van Bibber; 2006; Walsh, 2006). The federal government officially recognized that the CYI had ratified the agreement despite the Kaska's opposition, arguing that the CYI represented all Yukon First Nations in the comprehensive land claims process. In 1994 Parliament passed settlement legislation officially bringing the Umbrella Final Agreement and the first four Yukon First Nation Final and Self-Government Agreements into effect.

The Umbrella Final Agreement (UFA) is essential for understanding the Kwanlin Dün and Kaska claims because the UFA is the framework that each Yukon First Nation must use to negotiate its individual final agreement. The UFA specifies the amount of land quantum and financial compensation that each Yukon First Nation will receive upon completing its individual final agreement. It also sets out the range of powers and responsibilities that each Yukon First Nation can negotiate. These powers and responsibilities include: eligibility and enrolment, reserves and lands set aside, tenure and management of settlement lands, access, expropriation, surface rights board, settlement land amount, special management areas, land use planning, development assessment, heritage, water management, boundaries and measurements, fish and wildlife, forest resources, non-renewable resources, financial compensation, taxation, taxation of settlement land, economic development measures, resource royalty sharing, Yukon Indian self-government, transboundary agreements, dispute resolution, and implementation.

In essence, the UFA requires that all Yukon First Nations adopt its text for their final agreements. Each First Nation can, however, negotiate "specific provisions" that clarify or slightly modify the original text according to the unique circumstances of the First Nation. For instance, provision 13.8.3 of the Kwanlin Dün Final Agreement states that the "Government and the affected Yukon First Nation shall institute a permit system for research at any site which may contain Moveable Heritage Resources" (Kwanlin Dün First Nation Final Agreement, 2004: 186). This phrase is taken word for word from the UFA. Following this provision in the Kwanlin Dün agreement is a specific provision that states that the government and the Kwanlin Dün First Nation shall consult each other during the development and drafting of this permit system. It also describes the principles that must guide the government and the Kwanlin Dün in their construction of that permit system.

Two other points need to be mentioned about the UFA. First, the UFA was important because instead of the Whitehorse Indian Band signing the UFA, the Ta'an Kwäch'än First Nation and the Kwanlin Dün First Nation signed as separate First Nations. In 1998 INAC minister Jane Stewart officially separated these two First Nations by ministerial order, thus allowing them to negotiate their own individual final agreements under the UFA. Second, the Kaska were opposed to the UFA on both substantive and procedural grounds. In terms of the former, the Kaska had serious issues with the transboundary, taxation, trapping, extinguishment, land quantum, and repayment of loans chapters in the UFA. In terms of the latter, the Kaska felt that CYI did not properly ratify the UFA according to the UFA ratification provisions. Since the UFA ratification provisions were not properly followed, the Kaska maintain, the UFA was never officially ratified and therefore does not apply to their land claims negotiations (Dick, 2006; Dave Porter, 2006; Raider, 2006; Walsh, 2006).

During the final stages of the UFA negotiations in the early 1990s, some federal, territorial, and Yukon First Nations officials were becoming impatient with the land claims process. They felt that the process had been going on for far too long without producing any results. Therefore, the parties agreed to allow the CYI to identify four Yukon First Nations to begin negotiating individual agreements concurrently with the UFA negotiations (Joe, 2006; Koepke, 2006; McArthur, 2006; Mitander, 2006). The four that were chosen were Champagne/Aishihik, Nacho Nyak Dün, Teslin Tlingit, and Vuntut Gwitchin. Kwanlin Dün and the Kaska Nations were excluded from this initial list because theirs were seen as being potentially the most difficult negotiations in light of their complexities (described below). The first four Yukon First Nations to complete final agreements did so in 1995.

Also in 1995, the CYI decided to rewrite its constitution and rename itself the Council of Yukon First Nations (CYFN). Of the fourteen Yukon First Nations that belonged to the CYI, only eleven signed the new constitution. The three Yukon First Nations that refused to sign were the Kwanlin Dün First Nation, the Liard First Nation, and the Ross River Dena Council, meaning that these First Nations were no longer members of the CYFN. The Kaska pulled out of the CYFN because they opposed the CYI's handling of the UFA negotiations and ratification, while the Kwanlin Dün First Nation pulled out because it disagreed with the centralizing tendencies of the CYFN. Kwanlin Dün leaders also decided not to join the CYFN because of their past disagreements with CYI leaders over land claims issues and the CYI's position on the devolution of powers to the territorial government (Joe, 2006; Small, 2004).

After 1995, the federal and territorial governments began negotiating with all the Yukon First Nations at separate tables. Kwanlin Dün and Kaska negotiators initially made little progress as a result of the complex nature of their claims, described in greater detail below. Negotiations with all Yukon First Nations would speed up, however, as a result of the appointment of Bob Nault as minister of Indian and Northern Affairs Canada in 1999.[4] In April 2000, Nault announced that all Yukon comprehensive land claims negotiations had to be completed by 31 March 2002. Kwanlin Dün leaders and negotiators responded to the deadline with renewed vigour, eventually signing a memorandum of understanding with the federal and territorial governments to extend their negotiations beyond the deadline. In contrast, the Kaska negotiators failed to reach a memorandum of understanding before the deadline. As a result, they are currently without final agreements and their negotiations have been suspended since June 2002. The next section of this chapter looks at the Kwanlin Dün and Kaska negotiations in more detail before turning to an analysis of their divergent outcomes

Kwanlin Dün First Nation

→ *Little Progress: 1995 to 1999*

Kwanlin Dün final agreement negotiations commenced in late 1995, but very little progress was made until 1999. During these first four years, negotiations were hampered by three factors. First, government officials knew that Kwanlin Dün negotiations would be difficult and complex, so they decided to focus most of their efforts on those claims that they believed could be completed relatively quickly (Flynn, 2006; Armour, 2006; McCullough, 2006; King, 2006; Koepke, 2006; Beaudoin, 2006; Brown, 2006). Second, a number of anonymous sources have mentioned that a major obstacle to Kwanlin Dün negotiations during this period was a particular negotiator on the Kwanlin Dün team; informants described this negotiator as belligerent, hostile, and confrontational, making it impossible for negotiations to move forward beyond preliminary land selections. Finally, negotiations were hampered by the election of Joe Jack in 1996 as chief of Kwanlin Dün First Nation. One of his first moves as chief was to fire the entire staff of the land claims department, which in essence ended land claims negotiations with the federal and territorial governments. Moreover, Chief Jack's action sparked a series of intense and highly publicized confrontations between Jack's supporters and those of the fired land claims staff, paralysing the First Nation for three years (McNeely, 1998; Northern Native Broadcasting Yukon,[5] 1998; Northern Native Broadcasting Yukon, 1996; Parker, 1999b).

Towards an Agreement: 1999 to 2002 ←

The election of Rick O'Brien as chief of Kwanlin Dün First Nation in March 1999 was an important turning point because he was able to quell the political infighting that had plagued Kwanlin Dün since the mid-1990s. Moreover, O'Brien resurrected the land claims department and appointed a new department head, Tom Beaudoin, to restart land claims negotiations with the federal and territorial governments. In the eyes of federal and territorial officials, Beaudoin was a welcome relief from the previous team. He immediately put together a new negotiating team to restart negotiations. Members of his team included lawyer Keith Brown, consultant Lindsay Staples, and Kwanlin Dün citizen and lawyer Mike Smith, who had been chair of the CYI in the late 1980s and would later become chief of Kwanlin Dün First Nation in 2003.

By 1999, three Yukon First Nations (Little Salmon/Carmacks First Nation, Selkirk First Nation, and Tr'ondëk Hwëch'in First Nation), in addition to the original four, had completed individual final agreements. By the time Beaudoin's team was ready to restart negotiations in 1999, government negotiators felt they had completed enough of the other claims to begin focusing on the Kwanlin Dün. Rather than building on the work that the previous Kwanlin Dün negotiating team had accomplished during the mid-1990s, Beaudoin's team wanted to restart negotiations from scratch. To speed up the process, his team identified a number of crucial issues that the three negotiating parties had to resolve before a treaty could be completed: the inclusion of waterfront lands in Whitehorse as Settlement Lands, clarification of the First Nation's self-government powers in the city (e.g. land use planning), property taxation exemptions (because all land transferred under a treaty would immediately become taxable, which would probably bankrupt Kwanlin Dün), and the development of more robust economic measures (because Kwanlin Dün lands had limited fish, wildlife, and resource opportunities to generate economic development) (Beaudoin, 2006; Brown, 2006; Flynn, 2006; Koepke, 2006; King, 2006).

Although negotiators made decent progress during the first year of negotiations with Beaudoin's team, two events helped negotiations move forward. The first was the appointment of Bob Nault (August 1999 to December 2003) as minister of Indian and Northern Affairs Canada. In April 2000 Nault announced that the federal mandate to negotiate with the remaining Yukon First Nations would end on 31 March 2002 unless each of the tables could come to a memorandum of understanding to continue negotiations past the deadline (Tobin, 2000). Kwanlin Dün leaders and negotiators embraced the deadline as an opportunity to create pressure on themselves and on their government counterparts to complete a treaty.

The second event was the election of a progressive Whitehorse municipal council, led by Ernie Bourassa, mayor from 2000 to 2006. Throughout the course of Kwanlin Dün's negotiations, the City of Whitehorse had virtually no role in the negotiations. Although the city was allowed to send occasional representatives to observe negotiation sessions, it was not a formal participant. Rather, it was forced to rely on the territorial government to represent its interests (Armour, 2006; Bourassa, 2006; Flynn, 2006; McCullough, 2006; Stockdale, 2006). The city still had an important influence on YTG because a majority of the territory's population lived in Whitehorse. Indeed, the city was very important once negotiations were close to completion. One of the key issues for Kwanlin Dün leaders and negotiators was the inclusion of waterfront property as part of its Settlement Lands. Historically, as described earlier in the chapter, Kwanlin Dün members had spent significant amounts of time living on the banks of the Yukon River in Whitehorse. Unfortunately, the only available waterfront land in the city was owned by the. municipal government, which had purchased the former "Motorways trucking yard" property several years earlier. Previous city councils had been generally hostile to a Kwanlin Dün land claims agreement. However, the newly elected city council, led by Mayor Ernie Bourassa, was more receptive and was willing to dispose of the Motorways property as long as it was developed by the band to foster tourism. City officials liked Kwanlin Dün's plan to build a commercial office building, a retail building, a restaurant, a small hotel, and a cultural centre on the Motorways property. Therefore, the city agreed to sell the Motorways property to the territorial government so that it could then include it in the Kwanlin Dün treaty (Armour, 2006; Bourassa, 2006; Stockdale, 2006; Tobin, 2002b; Waddell, 2003).

A Final Agreement in Sight: 2002 to 2005

Several days before the 31 March 2002 deadline, Kwanlin Dün negotiators signed a memorandum of understanding with their government counterparts, thus settling all the major issues that the team had originally identified in 1999 (Beaudoin, 2006; Brown, 2006; Tobin, 2002a). With a completed MOU in hand, the negotiators spent the next year and a half finalizing and initialling the documents that would make up the Kwanlin Dün treaty. These documents included the final agreement, the self-government agreement, the implementation plans, and the ancillary agreements (Kwanlin Dün Programs and Services Transfer Agreements, Financial Transfer Agreement, and Kwanlin Dün Collateral Agreement).

In 2004 the Kwanlin Dün First Nation undertook an eight-month ratification process, beginning in March and ending with a referendum in November. The ratification vote involved two ballots, both of which had to be passed by a majority for the entire package to be ratified. Ballot 1 asked eligible beneficiaries aged eighteen years and over: "Do you approve of the Kwanlin Dün First Nation Final Agreement and the Memorandum Regarding Certain Financial and Other Arrangements?" Ballot 2 asked all eligible beneficiaries (eighteen and over) and all eligible members (eighteen and over) if they approved of the Kwanlin Dün First Nation self-government agreement, the dissolution of the Kwanlin Dün First Nation Band and the transferring of all its liabilities and assets to the Kwanlin Dün First Nation, the Kwanlin Dün First Nation Constitution, the Collateral Agreement, and the release of Kwanlin Dün's interest in two portions of Lot 226, a piece of the Range Road and a piece of the Takhini Trailer Park (Kwanlin Dün First Nation Ratification Committee, 2004: iii–v). The two ballots were necessary because the Kwanlin Dün Final Agreement only affected Kwanlin Dün beneficiaries ("traditional" members of Kwanlin Dün), while the other agreements (self-government, the constitution, collateral agreement, etc.) affected both beneficiaries (see above) and band members (who could be beneficiaries or "come from aways").

The results were as follows. On ballot 1 415 votes were cast out of a possible 468 (88.7% turnout). Of those 415 ballots, 254 voted yes (61.2%), 160 voted no (38.6%), and one ballot was rejected (0.02%). On ballot 2, two sets of ballots were counted separately. One set involved individuals who were beneficiaries and band members plus individuals who were beneficiaries but not band members. These were the same individuals who voted on ballot 1. Among these individuals, 414 votes were cast out of a possible 468 (88.5% turnout); 247 voted yes (59.7%), 161 voted no (38.8%), and 6 ballots were rejected (1.5%). The second set of ballots involved individuals who were beneficiaries and members plus individuals who were members but not beneficiaries. Among these individuals, 488 votes were cast out of a possible 563 (86.7% turnout); 292 voted yes (59.8%), 188 voted no (38.5%), and 8 ballots were rejected (1.6%). The "no" vote was relatively high, especially when compared to the Inuit ratification vote reported earlier in chapter 2. A possible explanation for the high "no" vote is presented below.

With a majority vote achieved on both ballots, the three negotiating parties formally signed the Kwanlin Dün treaty in a ceremony at Kwanlin Dün First Nation offices on 19 February 2005. At that signing ceremony, INAC minister Andy Scott and Grand Chief Ed Schultz of the Council of Yukon First Nations agreed that "to have a first nation of indigenous people with ownership of and control over significant parcels of land inside and outside a municipal boundary – nonetheless a capital city – is unique" (Tobin, 2005a). Highlights of the Kwanlin Dün First Nation treaty include:

- 647.5 square kilometres of Category "A" Settlement Land – Kwanlin Dün owns both the surface and sub-surface of these lands.
- 395.29 square kilometres of Category "B" Settlement Land – Kwanlin Dün First Nation owns only the surface of these lands.
- Lot 226, the Old Village, is designated Category "A" Settlement Land, but also keeps its Indian reserve status.
- Kwanlin Dün First Nation retains Aboriginal rights and titles to Category "A" and Category "B" Settlement Lands. It "cedes, releases, and surrenders" its rights and title to all Non-Settlement Lands and Fee Simple Settlement Land.
- 0.09 square kilometres of Fee Simple Settlement Land in Whitehorse.
- $46,974,502 in financial compensation over a period of fifteen years, tax free, plus a one-time payment of $6,391,381 to adjust the Kwanlin Dün First Nation compensation amount listed in the UFA for inflation.
- $24,171,070 in loans to be repaid by Kwanlin Dün First Nation to the federal government over fifteen years.
- Kwanlin Dün members continue to have access to Crown lands and can restrict access on Settlement Land subject to some exceptions.

- Government can expropriate Settlement Land for public purposes but must (1) try to avoid doing so as much as possible; (2) provide land or monetary compensation.
- Creation of Special Management Areas – Kusawa Park and Lewes Marsh Habitat Protection Area.
- Joint Land Use Planning between Kwanlin Dün and the territorial government.
- Heritage rights – specific provisions include money for a cultural centre, a waterfront heritage working group and plan, language and oral history promotion, and development of the Canyon City Historic Site.
- Water management rights.
- Fish and wildlife rights.
- Forest resources rights.
- Rights to non-renewable resources.
- Taxation Rights – s. 87 of the Indian Act will no longer exempt Kwanlin Dün members who receive income associated with reserve lands from paying income taxes.[6]
- Taxation of Settlement Land – specific provisions – Kwanlin Dün Settlement Lands operate under a set of different rules in light of the high value of their land selections.
- Economic measures – specific provisions – in light of the lack of fish and wildlife on Kwanlin Dün lands, the First Nation enjoys much stronger economic development rights than what are found in the other Yukon agreements.
- The right to negotiate a self-government agreement, which they did concurrently.
- Dispute resolution process. (Kwanlin Dün First Nation Final Agreement, 2004)

In general, the Kwanlin Dün Final Agreement is noteworthy on a number of fronts. First, although Kwanlin Dün received the smallest amount of Settlement Lands among the Yukon First Nations that concluded agreements, its lands have the potential to be the most valuable by virtue of being located in the territorial capital. Second, chapter 21 of the treaty on taxation of Settlement Lands is quite different from the other Yukon agreements in that it allows Kwanlin Dün Settlement Lands to remain tax free until the lands are developed or if certain time periods (usually between fifteen and twenty years) are reached (Flynn, 2006; Kwanlin Dün First Nation Final Agreement, 2004: 345). Third, the economic measures chapter gives the Kwanlin Dün government additional powers in light of the few fish and wildlife resources on its lands. These powers include a strategic economic development investment fund, the right to acquire up to a 25 per cent interest in resource and energy products, control over quarry leases, a plan to increase the number of Aboriginal government employees on Kwanlin Dün lands, the first right to acquire certain lands if the government decides to dispose of them, and the first right to acquire commercial freshwater fishing licences, commercial wilderness travel licences, game farming licences, fur farming licences, and outfitting concessions, among other powers (Kwanlin Dün First Nation Final Agreement, 2004).

The Kaska Final Agreement Negotiations

Despite their cultural, linguistic, and historical ties, Liard First Nation and Ross River Dena Council negotiated at separate tables until 1999. In 1987, members from the Kaska communities in the Yukon Territory and Northern British Columbia held their annual general assembly at Campbell River along the Robert Campbell Highway in the Yukon Territory, where they decided to recognize and give birth to the Kaska Nation (Dick, 2006; Dixon, 2006; McMillan, 2006; Van Bibber, 2006). To give expression to their new identity as one Kaska Nation, they created Kaska Tribal Council (KTC) in 1991 to conduct their treaty negotiations with the federal, territorial, and provincial governments. KTC's first and only hereditary chief thus far has been Hammond Dick and its only chief negotiator Dave Porter. Both men became the main land claims negotiators at the various Kaska tables in British Columbia and the Yukon. Ideally, KTC wanted to negotiate one agreement for all the Kaska claims. The federal government, however, refused (Dick, 2006; McMillan, 2006; Dave Porter, 2006; Raider, 2006; Walsh, 2006), mainly because they would not negotiate an agreement that had multiple subnational governments, that is, British Columbia and the Yukon Territory, as signatories.

After the ratification of the UFA in 1993 and the completion of the first four individual final agreements in 1995, negotiations with Liard First Nation and Ross River Dena Council began in late 1995. However, much like Kwanlin Dün negotiations, the Kaska negotiations moved very slowly as a result of the federal government's focus on those negotiations that it believed it could complete quickly. Government reluctance to negotiate with the Kaska stemmed from the Kaska's opposition to the UFA before the passing of federal settlement legislation in 1994, and the Kaska's insistence that the governments negotiate one Kaska deal at one table. In 1998 the federal government and the Kaska came to a compromise, agreeing to negotiate at one table for the Yukon Kaska First Nations, and at one table for the British Columbia Kaska First Nations. This change in federal position was probably the result of Bob Nault having just been appointed minister of INAC in 1999; Nault was determined to conclude the Yukon claims as quickly as possible (Hanson, 2006; King, 2006).

The Yukon Kaska negotiators identified a number of key issues that needed to be addressed. The first was the transboundary issue, the result of the Kaska claiming lands in the southeastern part of the Yukon and in the northern part of British Columbia. A second issue was the UFA's taxation chapter, which would require the Kaska to surrender their tax exemption status once they signed a treaty. Third, the Kaska wanted a commercial right to trap rather than just a subsistence right. Fourth, and most important, their treaty could not result in the "cede, release, and surrender" of their Aboriginal title. Fifth, Kaska negotiators wanted all negotiation loans forgiven because the amount of money they had borrowed was almost equal to the amount of financial compensation they were supposed to receive through their treaty. Finally, the Kaska wanted to renegotiate the amount of land quantum they were supposed to receive under the UFA. The UFA stated that Liard First Nation was to receive 930 square miles of Category "A" Settlement Land and 900 square miles of Fee Simple and Category "B" Settlement Land. Ross River Dena Council was to receive 920 square miles of "A" land and 900 square miles of Fee Simple and Category "B" land. The Yukon Kaska, however, wanted title to all of their traditional lands, which amounted to approximately 19,000 square miles of land in the Yukon and in British Columbia (Dick, 2006; Dixon, 2006; McMillan, 2006; Dennis Porter, 2006; Dave Porter, 2006; Raider, 2006; Van Bibber, 2006; Walsh, 2006).

Negotiations with the Kaska progressed relatively quickly once the federal government accepted the idea of a "Kaska Nation." They also accelerated because the federal government announced in April 2000 that its mandate to negotiate in the Yukon expired on 31 March 2002. In contrast to the Kwanlin Dün, the Kaska responded negatively, but continued to negotiate. They would later sue the federal government, arguing that the imposition of a two-year deadline was a breach of the federal government's duty to negotiate in good faith (Walsh, 2006). As a result, any new feelings of trust and goodwill built during these last rounds of negotiating quickly evaporated.

A couple of days before the 31 March 2002 deadline, Kaska negotiator Dave Porter's mother died. Out of respect for Porter, the federal minister extended the mandate of his negotiators until 21 June. Late in the evening on that day, the federal, territorial, and Kaska negotiators were able to agree to a tentative deal. Several days later, the KTC negotiating team presented the offer to Liard First Nation and Ross River Dena Council community members in a meeting in Watson Lake. At that meeting, the tentative deal was rejected forcefully by community leaders, members, and especially the elders, for reasons described below. One of the KTC officials suggested holding a referendum, but this was also rejected. According to federal and territorial officials, their governments never received a formal response from the Kaska regarding the tentative deal. However, government officials knew from media reports and from informal conversations with Kaska leaders that the deal was rejected by the membership. As a result, negotiations were formally ended in June 2002 and the Kaska immediately began a series of court cases against the federal government over the Crown's refusal to negotiate in good faith.

Very little is known about the tentative deal that was negotiated by the Kaska and the Crown in June 2002. All the officials involved politely refused to give me a copy of that tentative deal. Anonymous government officials did mention that the deal was similar to other completed final agreements, a fact that news media reports seem to confirm. A CBC online news report in August 2002 reported that the Kaska deal involved approximately 3800 square miles and $75 million in compensation and economic development funds (CBC, 2002). These numbers are similar to what the Liard First Nation and the Ross River Dena Council were supposed to receive under the UFA (3650 square, $40 million). Moreover, some interviewees indicated that the "cede, release, and surrender" provision was part of the tentative deal, as were the repayment of loans and the elimination of the Indian Act taxation exemption.

According to Kaska leaders and elders, the deal was rejected because it did not resolve the issues that the Kaska had raised in the early 1990s. Moreover, some Kaska informants maintained that the KTC negotiators had no right to agree to the tentative deal; by doing so, the negotiators had wilfully ignored the wishes of community leaders, elders, and members. Another leader claimed that the KTC officials have always been interested in negotiating because of the financial perks that they were receiving as negotiators.[7]

Today, some Kaska leaders remain interested in reopening negotiations. However, the majority of community leaders and members seem reluctant to reopen negotiations even if the federal government was willing to renew its negotiating mandate. After their land claims negotiations ended in June 2002, for instance, the Kaska initiated a number of lawsuits against the federal government. Furthermore, they negotiated two bilateral forestry agreements with the territorial government to facilitate resource development in their traditional territories. These agreements, in essence, gave the Kaska a veto over the co-management of forest resources in their traditional territories. Although these agreements have since lapsed, the Kaska maintain that the principles on which they were negotiated – a Kaska veto on Kaska traditional lands – continue to exist. Territorial government officials disagree, arguing that the veto died when the agreement lapsed. Current Liard First Nation leaders are very much interested in pursuing further bilateral agreements with the territorial government outside of the land claims process (McMillan, 2006; Dixon, 2006).

Explaining Divergent Outcomes

What explains the divergent outcomes of the Kwanlin Dün and the Kaska negotiations? The following section, as in the Labrador chapter, argues that four factors determine whether a comprehensive land claims agreement will be obtained: compatibility of goals, choice of tactics, Aboriginal group cohesion as it relates to treaty negotiations, and government perceptions of the Aboriginal group. The most important factor for the Yukon groups was the presence or lack of Aboriginal group cohesion as it related to treaty negotiations. Leadership was also crucial in the case of the KDFN.

Compatibility of Goals

As previously mentioned, "compatible goals" refers to the extent to which an Aboriginal group is willing to negotiate an agreement that is congruent with federal and provincial/territorial goals. In particular, it refers to the willingness of the Aboriginal group to accept a final agreement that operates within the political, economic, social, and legal contexts of the Canadian federation. As mentioned in previous chapters, compatible goals matter because the federal and the sub-national governments enjoy a significant advantage over Aboriginal participants in comprehensive land claims negotiations. As a result, an Aboriginal group will only be able to complete a treaty if it is willing to accept a final agreement that situates its administrative, legal, and self-governing institutions within the Canadian constitutional order.

Compatible versus incompatible goals were clearly important to the outcomes of the Kwanlin Dün and Kaska negotiations. Kwanlin Dün leaders and negotiators were willing to work within the terms of the UFA to negotiate a final agreement, whereas Kaska leaders were not. The Kwanlin Dün officials were also willing to share jurisdiction over lands located in Whitehorse and to accept a land quantum that was much less than the amount they had claimed in the past. Kaska leaders and community members, by contrast, were generally opposed to the permanent sharing or surrendering of any of their traditional lands.

A key driver of comprehensive land claims negotiations in the Yukon Territory was the federal government's desire to come to an agreement with *all* Yukon First Nations through some sort of collective process. As mentioned earlier in this chapter, one of the reasons why the Yukon First Nations' claims were the first to be accepted for active negotiations in 1975 was their willingness to work together with the federal government to negotiate a deal. This "one deal for all Yukon First Nations" approach has permeated negotiations since they began and came to fruition through the signing and ratification of the Umbrella Final Agreement (UFA) in 1993. For the federal and territorial governments, the UFA was a key step in Yukon land claims negotiations and is the only framework that can be used to negotiate individual final agreements (Koepke, 2006; Brown, 2006; Flynn, 2006; McCullough, 2006; Armour, 2006; Joe, 2006). In theoretical terms, the UFA is the only available framework for negotiating individual final agreements because of the "sunk costs" and "lock-in effects" that it has generated since 1993.[8] The federal and territorial governments are opposed to reopening the UFA because doing so would require renegotiating signed treaties. As such, the willingness of Aboriginal groups to work within the substantive framework of the UFA is a key factor in determining whether they can complete their final agreements.

Kwanlin Dün leaders have a long history of wanting to negotiate under some sort of Umbrella Agreement. In 1902 Jim Boss, a hereditary chief representing a variety of Indians from the Lake LaBerge area, submitted to the federal government a proposal to begin land claims negotiations (McClellan, 1987: 99). This proposal was the first known attempt in the Yukon by an Aboriginal group to pursue some sort of land claims treaty with the federal government (Coates, 1991: 163). In 1973 the Yukon First Nations statement of intent, *Together Today for Our Children Tomorrow*, was drafted and presented to the federal government by a number of Aboriginal leaders, the most prominent of whom was Whitehorse Indian Band chief Elijah Smith (McClellan, 1987: 95–6).[9] During more contemporary times, Kwanlin Dün members, such as Judy Gingell, former commissioner of the Yukon and also former chair of the Council for Yukon Indians, and Kwanlin Dün chiefs Pat Joe, Joe Jack, Rick O'Brien, and Mike Smith have all been interested in negotiating a final agreement within the framework of the UFA. Tom Beaudoin, who has been land claims director for the Kwanlin Dün since 1999, says that there was never any talk of scrapping or working outside the UFA (Beaudoin, 2006). Successive chiefs, councillors, and members of his negotiating team believed that although the UFA was not ideal, it was the best option they had since there was no alternative to it. Moreover, they felt that there was enough flexibility in the UFA to negotiate a final agreement that would meet the particular needs of the Kwanlin Dün. For instance, the key issues of waterfront lands, self-government powers in Whitehorse, property taxation, and stronger economic powers were all capable of being addressed within the UFA in a way that satisfied Kwanlin Dün leaders and negotiators. Moreover, although the band's land quantum was one of the smallest among the Yukon First Nations, the amount was acceptable since its lands were located in Whitehorse, making them potentially the most valuable lands in the territory (Beaudoin, 2006; Brown, 2006).

The Kaska, by contrast, have been much more hostile towards the UFA.[10] In general, Kaska leaders and community members believe that the UFA has failed to address the issues that are unique and are of utmost importance to them. In particular, they take issue with the fact that chapter 25 of the UFA gives the territorial government a veto over negotiations that involve transboundary issues. They are also opposed to chapter 20.6, which states that the tax-exemption provisions in the Indian Act no longer apply once a final agreement is completed. Chapter 16, regarding the right to trap, is in their view insufficient because it only allows signatory members to trap for subsistence; the Kaska believe that they have a right to trap for commercial purposes. They are also opposed to the "cede, release, and surrender" clauses in chapters

4 and 5, the repayment of comprehensive land claim negotiation loans, and the amount of land quantum they are supposed to receive under the UFA (McMillan, 2006; Dennis Porter, 2006; Dave Porter, 2006; Raider, 2006; Van Bibber 2006; Walsh, 2006).

These final two issues are particular sore points for Kaska leaders and band members. In terms of the first issue, the amount of money that the federal government has loaned to the Kaska for land claims negotiations will soon match the amount of compensation monies that they were supposed to receive in a Final Agreement. This situation means that even if Kaska negotiators and leaders were able to complete a treaty, they would face a shortage in financial resources to successfully engage in economic development, the provision of services, and the construction of community projects, infrastructure, and housing (Dixon, 2006; Dave Porter, 2006; Sterriah, 2006; Walsh, 2006). The second issue of land quantum is clearly the most important among the majority of Kaska members. Having spoken to a number of community members, leaders, and elders in Ross River and Liard First Nation, I conclude that guaranteed ownership of a substantial percentage of their traditional lands is needed before Kaska members will agree to any deal. According to Steve Walsh (2006), Kaska Nation lawyer and honorary member, the Umbrella Agreement simply does not offer enough land, especially in light of what other Aboriginal groups across Canada have received. For instance, the federal government offered 14 square miles per person in the Inuvialiut agreement; it offered the Deh Cho 7 square miles per person, while the Yukon First Nations got 2 square miles per person (Walsh, 2006). According to Norman Sterriah (2006), former chief of Ross River and a land claims negotiator, the Kaska must have control over the majority of their traditional territories, including the valuable mineral and forest resources. Liard First Nation elder Eileen Van Bibber (2006) argues that all the Kaska's traditional lands are important. The Kaska are one of the most traditional groups in the Yukon, with many community members spending significant amounts of time out on the land. In Van Bibber's view, the UFA does not provide enough land to match the cultural needs of the Kaska. According to Van Bibber and a number of other Kaska elders, the land offered by the federal government could be traversed in a day by dogsled, an amount that is simply unacceptable in light of the cultural needs of the Kaska.

Kaska concerns with the UFA are not limited to its contents. Leaders, members, and the negotiators also challenge the validity of its ratification, arguing that it was never properly ratified according to UFA provisions (Dave Porter 2006; Raider, 2006; Sterriah, 2006; Walsh 2006). Chapter 2.2.8 of the Umbrella Agreement reads: "The parties to the Umbrella Final Agreement shall negotiate the processes for ratification of the Umbrella Final Agreement and the ratification of those processes shall be sought at the same time as ratification of the Umbrella Final Agreement." According to Kaska informants, however, this ratification process was never followed. Rather, on 31 March 1993 the Council of Yukon Indians held its usual quarterly board meeting, and at that meeting the representatives of the various Yukon First Nations passed a motion to ratify the Umbrella Final Agreement. The representatives from Ross River and Liard First Nation protested the ratification process and voted against ratification; however, the motion carried. The position of the Kaska, therefore, is that since proper procedures for ratifying the UFA were never carried out, and since the Kaska voted no to ratification, the UFA does not apply to them (Dick, 2006; Raider, 2006; Walsh, 2006; Dave Porter, 2006). According to several Aboriginal and government officials who were involved in the negotiation and ratification of the Umbrella Final Agreement, Yukon First Nation leaders were not concerned about the UFA's ratification procedure since they thought all the Yukon First Nations would eventually sign Final Agreements anyway, making the issue moot.[11] The Kaska reject the UFA and have been demanding a new negotiating process that allows them to negotiate a final agreement that substantially deviates from the UFA. The federal and territorial governments, however, have refused to negotiate under any other framework.

Another example of the role that compatible goals versus incompatible goals plays relates to the willingness of Kwanlin Dün and Kaska leaders, negotiators, and community members to share permanent jurisdiction over some of their lands with the federal, territorial, and municipal governments. One of the reasons why Kwanlin Dün negotiations took so long was because its proposed settlement lands were located within the municipal boundaries of Whitehorse. There was tension between Kwanlin Dün interests, on the one hand, and city interests, on the other. City officials were very much concerned about the possibility of a patchwork of Kwanlin Dün and municipal by-laws operating within municipal boundaries. Some non-Aboriginal Whitehorse residents were apprehensive about being subject to Kwanlin Dün laws and Kwanlin Dün law enforcement officers. In response to these concerns, Kwanlin Dün negotiators agreed to adopt territorial and city laws of general application on their settlement lands within the municipal boundaries of Whitehorse. Moreover, they agreed to allow city officials to enforce those laws. The negotiating parties also cooperated with regard to zoning, planning, and land use regulations. For land use designations, for instance, the parties agreed to negotiate jointly designations for each parcel of settlement land (approximately eighty parcels) that came into contact with municipal property. If Kwanlin Dün owned a parcel of land that was located next to a city residential parcel, then the parties could agree to designate the Kwanlin Dün parcel as "residential." Therefore, Kwanlin Dün could do what it pleased with the parcel as long as the use of the land fit into the broad category of "residential." (Flynn, 2006; Kwanlin Dün First Nation Final Agreement, 2004: chapter 11).

In short, Kwanlin Dün negotiations were facilitated by the willingness of its leaders and negotiators to negotiate an agreement that was compatible with government goals. Further evidence of the importance of compatible goals is in the willingness of Kwanlin Dün negotiators to accept the 1036 square kilometres of land quantum listed in the UFA (Kwanlin Dün First Nation Final Agreement, 2004: 100). According to government and First Nation participants in the negotiations, there was never any mention of renegotiating this amount. There was also never any discussion of asserting Kwanlin Dün First Nation sovereignty or renegotiating the certainty/surrender provisions outlined in the UFA (Beaudoin, 2006; Brown, 2006; Koepke, 2006).

Contrast these views and experiences with those of the Kaska. Kaska leaders and community members in Liard First Nation and especially in Ross River have very strong feelings about Kaska sovereignty and Kaska nationhood (Bi-Lateral Agreement between the Kaska and the Yukon Government, 2003; Tobin, 2003b). Hammond Dick (2006), Kaska tribal council chief, has stated that "cede, release, and surrender" of their traditional lands is not an option and is a major barrier to negotiations proceeding. He argues that it is unfair that the Kaska must adopt this clause when the bands in British Columbia do not have to do so. According to Eileen Van Bibber (2006), an influential Kaska elder, in 1973 the Kaska originally asked for 19,000 square miles of land. When the Yukon First Nations leaders returned from Ottawa, they brought back an offer of 16,000 square miles to be shared among *all* the Yukon First Nations. For her, nothing short of a substantial amount of their original demand of 19,000 square miles will be acceptable for the completion of their land claim. Others, such as Kaska lawyer Steve Walsh (2006), Chief Liard McMillan (2006), and former chief Norman Sterriah

(2006), agree that nothing short of formal recognition of their title to most, if not all, of their traditional lands, will be acceptable. The Kaska's strong opposition to surrender is confirmed by federal and territorial officials (Armour, 2006; Hanson, 2006; Koepke, 2006; McCullough, 2006).

This is not to say that the Kaska are completely unwilling to share their lands and their jurisdictions with the federal and territorial governments. In the past, they have been willing to temporarily share their traditional lands with the territorial government for the purposes of economic development. However, the Kaska have made it clear that their consent is needed for any developments on their lands; they maintain sovereignty over all their lands until a land claims agreement is negotiated (Dave Porter, 2006; Walsh, 2006; Sterriah, 2006). For instance, in May 2003 the Kaska and the Yukon government negotiated a bilateral agreement separate from land claims negotiations that allowed the territorial government to undertake economic development on Kaska lands for a two-year period (Barichello, 2006). The preamble of this bilateral agreement states that "Yukon acknowledged, in agreements entered into with the Kaska in January 1997, that the Kaska have Aboriginal rights, titles and interest in and to the Kaska Traditional Territory in the Yukon" (Bi-Lateral Agreement, 2003: 1). Section 3 of this agreement, entitled "Kaska Consent," states that any dispositions of interests in lands or resources in Kaska traditional territory cannot be given "without consulting and obtaining the consent of the Kaska" (ibid.: 4). The point here is that the Kaska are willing to share jurisdiction of their land, but only on a temporary basis; a final agreement must recognize their Aboriginal title, not extinguish it. They maintain this position because of their experiences in the past where the federal and territorial governments engaged in development on their lands (like the mine in Faro) without their consent.

Tactics

In addition to compatible goals, the choice of tactics during negotiations affects whether a land claim will be completed. In essence, those groups that focus on negotiations tend to complete land claims agreements. Those groups that mix negotiating with confrontational tactics such as protests and litigation tend not to complete land claims agreements. Moreover, the frequency with which the Kwanlin Dün and the Kaska negotiators engaged in community consultations also mattered.

The Kwanlin Dün First Nation has a long history of focusing on negotiations, from Jim Boss in 1902 until the present. It has rarely used confrontational tactics, especially since Tom Beaudoin's team took over the land claims department in 1999 (Beaudoin, 2006; Brown, 2006; King, 2006; Hanson, 2006). The only litigation that the Kwanlin Dün First Nation has engaged in since 1973 was the court case over whether Lot 226, the Old Village, qualified as an Indian reserve. This court case, however, was completely separate from land claims negotiations and had no impact on them (Flynn, 2006; McCullough, 2006; Armour, 2006; Beaudoin, 2006; King, 2006). Indeed, according to a number of anonymous interviewees, the Kwanlin Dün sued the government over Lot 226 only because it was counselled to do so by a lawyer who has a reputation for advocating litigation.

The Kwanlin Dün First Nation did hold some protests during its negotiations, but this was before 1999, under a different lands claims director. Moreover, according to a former employee, under that director the protests were more like "celebrations." The idea was to invite community members from Kwanlin Dün and Whitehorse to a fish fry or barbecue on lands that Kwanlin Dün was interested in including in its treaty. Kwanlin Dün "protests" were basically informational campaigns designed to create positive feelings among Whitehorse citizens towards Kwanlin Dün land claims. They were not the type of protests that the Innu in Labrador, for instance, have undertaken.

The Kaska, by contrast, have used a mix of negotiations and litigation. Dave Porter, their chief negotiator, has always been interested in negotiating a land claim. At the same time, however, the Kaska have a long history of suing the federal government over land claims–related issues. Since 1986 they have sued the federal government eight times (see, for instance, Small, 2002a; Whitehorse Daily Star Staff Writers, 2001; Tobin, 2003c; Tobin, 2003a; O'Grady, 2005).[12] One of the many cases they have against the federal government has to do with the 1870 British "Order in Council Transferring Rupert's Land and the North-Western Territories to Canada." This order formally brought the Yukon Territory into the Canadian federation. Of particular note is schedule A, a letter "from the Senate and House of Commons of the Dominion of Canada" to the Queen of England. It states: "And furthermore, ... upon the transference of the territories in question to the Canadian Government, the claims of the Indian tribes to compensation for lands required for purposes of settlement will be considered and settled in conformity with the equitable principles which have uniformly governed the British Crown in its dealings with the aborigines" (Cameron and Gomme, 1991: 35). In essence, schedule A of the 1870 order commits the federal government to use equitable principles to consider, settle, and compensate Yukon First Nations for any lands the government uses for settlement. The Kaska have read this schedule to mean that the federal government must not only negotiate with them in good faith using equitable principles, but must also provide compensation to the Kaska for any use of their traditional lands. In particular, the Kaska want the federal government to pay them monetary compensation for what they see as illegal mining and forestry activities on their lands since 1870 (Dave Porter, 2006; Sterriah, 2006; Walsh, 2006).

Other litigation has argued that the federal government breached its duty to negotiate in good faith when it imposed the 31 March 2002 deadline on land claims negotiations in the Yukon. The Kaska lawyer argues that the 1870 order is the only constitutional document in Canada that requires the federal government to sign treaties with the First Nations before their lands can be settled and developed. The Kaska have also sued the federal government over the illegal ratification of the UFA (Walsh, 2006). The constant stream of Kaska litigation has greatly hampered negotiations by fostering negative relations between negotiators and leaders and confusing band members who see their representatives negotiating a treaty but also litigating on and off at the same time.

In contrast to the Labrador cases, one tactical difference that emerged in the Yukon cases was the frequency with which the two Yukon groups undertook community consultations. Before 1999, the Kwanlin Dün First Nation land claims team held negotiations in Kwanlin Dün government offices, opening them up to any band members who wished to attend. Moreover, the land claims department held frequent consultations with community members on the progress of its negotiations. According to a number of those who participated in negotiations during this time period, negotiations tended to proceed slowly as a direct result of community participation. Holding negotiations in Kwanlin Dün government offices and inviting community members to attend negotiation sessions created a lot of distractions for the negotiating teams. In 1997 the Kwanlin Dün land claims department was closed down due to political infighting. After the election of Chief Rick O'Brien in March 1999, the department was reopened, with Tom Beaudoin as its head. One of the first things that Beaudoin did was reduce the number of community consultation exercises. More important, he moved the site of negotiations from

Kwanlin Dün offices to territorial government offices in Whitehorse. The idea was to reduce the distractions that the previous negotiators had faced when negotiations were held in Kwanlin Dün offices (Beaudoin, 2006). According to Kwanlin Dün and territorial officials, holding negotiations in Yukon territorial offices had a positive effect on the speed and direction of Kwanlin Dün Final Agreement negotiations (Beaudoin, 2006; Flynn, 2006; McCullough, 2006; Armour, 2006; Brown, 2006; King, 2006). The Kwanlin Dün's successful decision to limit consultations during negotiations can be explained by the difficulty of negotiating when mass input is required (see Lustig, 1994). This is not to say that community consultations did not occur. In fact, during the Kwanlin Dün Final Agreement ratification process, the land claims department undertook a massive information campaign, distributing information leaflets, holding community meetings, doing radio interviews, and engaging in other informational activities. The First Nation also took more time to ratify the agreement to ensure that the membership fully understood its provisions (Beaudoin, 2006; Brown, 2006; Tobin, 2004b). The point here is that the land claims department limited community involvement and the distribution of information somewhat until the ratification period started. This strategy allowed the Kwanlin Dün to negotiate a deal relatively free from distractions and is something that the Labrador Innu have started to do since 2002. Moreover, increasing the time period and the level of community involvement during the ratification process allowed Kwanlin Dün leaders to build enough support to ratify the treaty (Beaudoin, 2006; Brown, 2006).[13]

The Kaska, by contrast, have always had and still maintain substantial community involvement in negotiations. According to former Liard First Nation chief Ann Maje Raider (2006), and others (Dick, 2006; Dennis Porter, 2006; Sterriah, 2006; Van Bibber, 2006), Kaska members are very vocal about being at the table during negotiations. There is a strong feeling among the grassroots that Kaska leaders cannot agree to anything unless they have a clear mandate from the membership and have a substantial number of grassroots members in attendance at negotiation meetings. Moreover, public meetings are always well attended, although some members, especially the elders, have difficulty understanding key issues and concepts. For instance, many Kaska elders and members tend to link "cede, release, and surrender" to monetary compensation; in other words, they believe that a land claim is simply an exchange of their lands for money (Dick, 2006; Dixon, 2006; Dennis Porter, 2006; Van Bibber, 2006).

According to territorial officials (Armour, 2006; McCullough, 2006), when negotiations are held in Ross River or Watson Lake, meetings sometimes end up addressing issues that have nothing to do with land claims. For instance, during negotiation sessions in Ross River, some Kaska members have asked questions that relate to their immediate social, economic, and political problems. At one meeting on fish and wildlife, a Kaska member asked a question about his current problems with housing. For the Kaska, their tradition of intense public involvement has tended to hinder land claims negotiations.

It is unclear whether "community consultation" is a key component of the tactics factor. The Innu and the Inuit case studies in Labrador did not indicate that "community consultations" were an important aspect of tactics that affected their outcomes, although recent developments on the Innu side may change this assessment. Rather, in all four case studies, the key aspect of tactics was the degree to which the Aboriginal group minimized or maximized the use of confrontational strategies. Still, it is useful to point out the possible effect that "community consultations" can have on outcomes. It may be something that Aboriginal leaders can use to affect negotiations.

Internal Cohesion as It Relates to Treaty Negotiations

Much like the Labrador cases, internal cohesion as it relates to treaty negotiations was a factor for the Yukon cases. Similarly, internal cohesion dynamics for the Kwanlin Dün and the Kaska were affected by their historical interactions with federal and territorial agencies. Internal cohesion affected Kwanlin Dün and Kaska land claims negotiations in two ways. First, the way in which the two groups dealt with the dynamics of internal group competition affected the way that their respective negotiation paths progressed. Second, although both groups suffered from significant internal social, economic, and political problems, they differed in how they addressed them in terms of their impact on their comprehensive land claims negotiations.

One of the reasons why the Kwanlin Dün was one of the last groups to complete a deal was the internal dynamics of the First Nation. Historically, as described earlier in the chapter, the Kwanlin Dün First Nation was the Whitehorse Indian Band, created by Indian and Northern Affairs Canada in 1956 (Whitehorse Daily Star Staff Writers, 1998). As such, the Whitehorse Indian Band was in fact an amalgam of traditional Kwanlin Dün and Ta'an Kwäch'än peoples, as well as any status Indians who had decided to relocate and live in Whitehorse. These "come from aways" were not traditional members of the Whitehorse Indian Band, but were considered band members for the purposes of delivering Indian Affairs programs and services (INAC, 2005; Koepke, 2006; Beaudoin, 2006; Brown, 2006).

As a result of this diversity, created by the federal government, comprehensive land claims negotiations have always been complex for the Kwanlin Dün. The traditional members from Kwanlin Dün generally have different interests and traditions than the members from Ta'an Kwäch'än, despite several decades of living together under the Whitehorse Indian Band designation. More important, "come from aways" have traditionally had little interest in the band's comprehensive land claims negotiations because many of them are beneficiaries of other Yukon First Nations.[14] These divisions made it difficult for the Kwanlin Dün's land claims department before the appointment of Tom Beaudoin to present clear and representative positions at the negotiating table. Prospects for completing a final agreement improved in 1993 when the Ta'an Kwäch'än and the Kwanlin Dün First Nations were listed as separate First Nation signatories to the Umbrella Final Agreement. In 1998 the Ta'an Kwäch'än First Nation formally separated from the Kwanlin Dün under a ministerial order by then–Indian Affairs minister Jane Stewart (Whitehorse Daily Star Staff Writers, 1998; Northern Native Broadcasting Yukon, 1998). By removing Ta'an Kwäch'än members from the Kwanlin Dün table, Kwanlin Dün officials now only had to deal with the "come from aways," who were largely indifferent to whether the Kwanlin Dün completed a deal. As a result, the prospects for completing a Kwanlin Dün treaty dramatically improved.

The Kaska, by contrast, took the opposite approach. At the outset of negotiations, Liard First Nation and Ross River Dena Council negotiated separately. That situation changed after 1987. In that year the Kaska communities of Ross River (Yukon Territory), Liard First Nation (Yukon Territory), Dease River First Nation (British Columbia), Lower Post First Nation (British Columbia), and Fort Ware Band (British Columbia) gathered at Campbell River, in between Ross River and Watson Lake in the Yukon Territory, to form the Kaska Nation. The governing body of the Kaska Nation was the Kaska Tribal Council (KTC), a not-for-profit organization and BC-registered society that served as a de facto government representing all Kaska at the negotiating table (Dick, 2006; McMillan, 2006; Van Bibber, 2006).

Negotiating at one table has proved to be a problematic strategy for the Kaska. The federal and territorial governments have refused to negotiate one deal for the Kaska Nation. As well, each community has different interests in completing a treaty. At different times, some groups have been more interested; at other times, they have lost interest (Armour, 2006; Barichello, 2006). Tim Koepke (2006), chief federal negotiator, agrees that the one Kaska Nation approach has sometimes made it difficult to get a deal done. It is unclear to government negotiators which communities are being represented at the table, and which are not. It is unclear which communities support certain provisions, and which do not. Moreover, individual Kaska communities seem to have mixed feelings about the Kaska Tribal Council; sometimes a community will demand individual consultation on certain negotiation issues, whereas at other times it will defer to the KTC. From 1995 to 1998, for instance, Liard First Nation informally pulled away from KTC to undertake its own land claims negotiations with the two governments (Sterriah, 2006). The band adopted this strategy on the advice of an external negotiator who recommended that the band negotiate on its own, separate from the KTC. When this negotiator left Liard First Nation, and the federal and territorial governments agreed to negotiate a deal with KTC at two tables (one for the Yukon and one for British Columbia), Liard First Nation returned to the KTC umbrella.

Two other aspects of internal cohesion, community social problems and political infighting, have affected negotiations. In general, both Aboriginal groups suffer from substance abuse and unemployment problems. However, the Kaska face more significant problems than the Kwanlin Dün, probably because Kwanlin Dün members have access to greater economic opportunities in Whitehorse.[15] According to the "Community Wellbeing Index" generated by Indian and Northern Affairs Canada's Research and Analysis Directorate, both Kaska Nations were among the poorest among Yukon First Nations in terms of income, education, labour force activity, and housing conditions (INAC, 2007). Interviewees confirmed these findings. Former Yukon premier Tony Penikett [interview] (2006) mentioned that the Kaska suffer from severe poverty and rampant substance abuse, and rely heavily on a subsistence economy. Norman Barichello (2006), a land claims negotiator who worked for the Kaska, describes Ross River as having a notorious reputation both inside and outside the community for significant alcohol and drug abuse problems. Former Ross River chief and land claims negotiator Norman Sterriah (2006) agrees that both Yukon Kaska communities, but especially Ross River, suffer from significant social and economic problems. Others, like former federal regional director of INAC in the Yukon Elizabeth Hanson (2006), Yukon government officials Karyn Armour (2006) and Lesley McCullough (2006), Kaska Tribal Council chief Hammond Dick (2006), Liard First Nation chief Liard McMillan (2006), and Kaska negotiator Steve Walsh (2006) all confirm that the Kaska suffer from greater social and economic problems than the Kwanlin Dün (see also Tobin, 17 March 2004).

These problems have distracted the Kaska from maintaining focus on land claims negotiations. According to Yukon government officials, meetings held in Ross River to discuss land claims issues had a tendency to shift from land claims discussions to proposals for addressing the social and economic problems of the community (Armour, 2006; McCullough, 2006). Current Ross River chief Jack Caesar and Liard First Nation chief Liard McMillan (2006) both were elected on platforms that stressed community healing and self-reliance as opposed to land claims negotiations. Previous chiefs like Norman Sterriah (2006) and Anne Raider (2006) also found themselves constantly trying to juggle land claims negotiations and non–land claims solutions to the significant social problems of both communities. The key point here is that social and economic problems were front and centre during Kaska negotiations, making a treaty settlement more difficult to accomplish.

In addition to social and economic problems at the community level, both Aboriginal groups have a history of political infighting. Of the two, the Kwanlin Dün First Nation has had to deal with more intense rivalries and politicking for most of its history, especially from 1956 onwards after the creation of the Whitehorse Indian Band (Northern Native Broadcasting Yukon, 1998; Tobin, 1999b). Infighting was at its highest during the 1980s and 1990s as political squabbles emerged along family lines. In 1985 three councillors tried to oust Chief Johnny Smith because of allegations of corruption regarding his administration of the band's development corporation, election fixing, and the appointment of band employees on the basis of family connections. In the late 1980s Chief Ann Smith was accused of corruption due to the presence of illegal ballots. Her successor, Lena Johns, also faced allegations of corruption; Johns also had to deal with the defeat of her proposed band constitution and faced a divisive re-election campaign. In 1996 Joe Jack was elected chief of Kwanlin Dün and immediately fired Pat Joe from her job as land claims director. In response, Pat Joe allied with two band councillors to try to oust Joe Jack for illegally firing her (McNeely, 1998; Northern Native Broadcasting Yukon, 1996). This dispute evolved into a larger political struggle between Pat Joe's minority faction and Chief Jack's majority faction on the council, paralysing the First Nation. In 1997 the Bank of Nova Scotia informed the band that it would not be releasing any of the band's money to the council because it was unsure which faction had legitimate signing authority (Northern Native Broadcasting Yukon, 1998; Parker, 1999b). The dispute was eventually resolved with the election of Rick O'Brien as chief in March 1999 (Tobin, 1999c).

Although both groups suffered from social and economic problems and political infighting, only the Kaska negotiations were affected significantly by them. The fact that Kaska negotiations were the only ones hampered by these problems is surprising, since the Kwanlin Dün have a long history of intense political dysfunction. The key difference between the divergent experiences of these two groups was leadership. Kaska leaders have historically been divided on whether to negotiate a land claims agreement. Kaska Tribal Council leaders like chief negotiator Dave Porter and, to a lesser extent, Kaska Tribal Council chief Hammond Dick have been interested in negotiating a deal, and draw their support from those who want a treaty. However, community leaders have been less enthusiastic. Dixon Lutz, the hereditary chief of Liard First Nation, has long been reluctant about a land claims deal (Van Bibber, 2006). Current elected band council chiefs Jack Caesar and Liard McMillan have both stated they are not interested in land claims negotiations. Many Kaska members have mentioned that elders have been the most vocal in opposing a land claims agreement. The opinions of Kaska elders are especially significant since the Kaska are one of the most traditional groups in the Yukon; they continue to venerate elders as their primary sources of knowledge, leadership, and influence.

Disagreement among leaders regarding land claims is best illustrated by an event in June 2002, when Dave Porter brought a tentative deal with the governments to a Kaska community meeting in Watson Lake. At that meeting, Dave Porter and Hammond Dick tried to push the community to accept the deal, or at least put it up to a vote. Local leaders, community members, and most of the elders, however, were very much opposed to the deal, and as a result the deal was rejected without a vote being held (Barichello, 2006; McMillan, 2006; Dave Porter, 2006; Sterriah, 2006; Van Bibber, 2006; Walsh, 2006).

In sum, internal cohesion with respect to whether leaders and community members want a deal can have a great effect on whether a land claims agreement is completed. Lack of internal cohesion on this issue indicates that leaders may be working at cross purposes, with community leaders (like band councillors and band chiefs) focusing on community problems outside of land claims negotiations, and Kaska Tribal Council leaders focusing on land claims as the solution to community problems. Disagreement effects are also felt at the negotiating table, where government negotiators question whether Kaska negotiators have a mandate to negotiate. They also wonder which communities are opposed and which are supportive of certain negotiated provisions and positions.

Contrast these experiences with the Kwanlin Dün. As mentioned above, the Kwanlin Dün First Nation has a long history of political infighting, especially from the mid-1980s to the late 1990s, with very little getting done. Despite these internal cohesion problems, the KDFN was able to complete its treaty for two reasons. First, the political infighting that plagued the First Nation in the 1980s and 1990s was not over whether to engage in land claims negotiations. Rather, the disputes were between certain families struggling for control over the band council. All these leaders, however, supported land claims negotiations. As I have stressed throughout this book, the Kwanlin Dün has a long history of leaders who have supported negotiating a land claims agreement.

Second, the election of Rick O'Brien as chief of Kwanlin Dün on 23 March 1999 was a turning point because he was able to bridge the rival factions. His campaign platform was to promote "unity among Kwanlin Dün members who've been divided by political differences over the last three years and longer." Moreover, he believed that "reigniting Kwanlin Dün's land claim negotiations is also of the utmost importance" (Tobin, 1999c). Most important, he was not connected to either of the competing factions, and thus ran as a neutral candidate who could put an end to the political infighting. Once he was elected, the political rivalries that had plagued the band for years were subdued. In addition to ending the political infighting, O'Brien revived Kwanlin Dün's land claims department by hiring a new director (Tom Beaudoin) to form a new negotiating team. He also gave the department a mandate and the necessary political support to actively negotiate a completed agreement (Beaudoin, 2006; Brown, 2006).

In short, KDFN members and leaders have long supported the idea of a modern treaty, but political infighting had prevented negotiations from progressing. The election of Rick O'Brien helped to end the infighting and allowed the membership and leadership to focus on completing a settlement agreement. Near the end of his term, O'Brien decided to leave KDFN politics for a job with the Council of Yukon First Nations. Mike Smith, a band member and KDFN negotiator, replaced Rick O'Brien as KDFN chief in 2003, ensuring that KDFN leadership remained focused on the goal of a completed land claims settlement (Small, 2003b).

Government Perceptions of the Aboriginal Groups

Government perceptions also had a role in determining the divergent outcomes that the Kaska and the Kwanlin Dün First Nations experienced in their negotiations. In general, federal and territorial officials have negative perceptions of the Kaska and more positive perceptions of the Kwanlin Dün. As in the above analysis on internal cohesion, leadership was important for helping the Kwanlin Dün establish positive government perceptions despite the group's history of political discord.

In general, government officials have doubts regarding whether the Kaska First Nations can be financially accountable. For instance, both Kaska communities have been at various times under remedial management (in which the federal government oversees the activities of the band council) due to their difficulties in managing their financial affairs (Koepke, 2006). Under former chief Daniel Morris, Liard First Nation was investigated for illegally lending band money to band members, failing to maintain proper bookkeeping practices, and refusing to remit $1.5 million in income taxes to the federal government (Brown, 2003; CBC, 2006b; Tobin, 2005b). Current chief Liard McMillan, who succeeded Daniel Morris, has faced protests from community members who have charged that his administration is not transparent and accountable. In particular, he has been criticized for failing to hold regular band council meetings, for not giving full disclosure of the band's program spending, and for not informing members of the capital plans of a new corporation that the band created (CBC, 2006b). At the same time, his band council has struggled with what it describes as a "significant cash-flow problem," which resulted in layoffs and cutbacks in March 2005. The Department of Indian and Northern Affairs closely monitored the situation to ensure that federal programs and services continued to be offered to Kaska community members (Tobin, 15 March 2005). The point here is that federal and territorial officials have concerns regarding the ability of the Kaska groups to govern effectively under a final agreement.

In addition, as mentioned above, federal and territorial governments today are unsure as to whether the Kaska people are indeed interested in a deal (Armour, 2006; Flynn, 2006; Hanson, 2006; McArthur, 2006; McCullough, 2006). Although the Kaska negotiating team, led by Dave Porter, is very much interested in negotiating a deal, band council leaders, elders, and community members seem to be reluctant to do so. Band council leaders have historically shown more interest in dealing with community-level issues. Over time, elders and community members have become less and less interested in a land claims agreement. Once elders and members understood that a final agreement would lead to the extinguishment of their title, public opinion within the Kaska communities quickly shifted to passive opposition. Also influencing local leaders and members were the experiences of members from other Yukon First Nations that had completed final agreements. Most of the Kaska members I spoke to mentioned how these other members were telling them not to sign an agreement. The result is that federal and provincial officials are unsure of the Kaska's position on land claims because there seems to be disunity between Kaska Tribal Council leaders like Dave Porter and Hammond Dick[16] and local leaders like chiefs, band council members, and elders.

Kwanlin Dün also initially suffered from negative government perceptions that stemmed from the KDFN's long history of political dysfunction, as discussed above (Beaudoin, 2006; King, 2006; Northern Native Broadcasting Yukon, 1996; Northern Native Broadcasting Yukon, 1997). Kwanlin Dün disputes have long been highly publicized and consistently reported in territorial newspapers and television newscasts (see, for instance, McNeely, 1998; Northern Native Broadcasting Yukon, 1997; Parker, 1999a; Tobin, 1999a). These disputes sometimes spilled into federal jurisdiction, with various factions calling on the minister of Indian and Northern Affairs to resolve their disputes. For instance, the dispute between Pat Joe and Joe Jack involved an appeal to Minister Jane Stewart in 1998 to step in and adjudicate their dispute (Northern Native Broadcasting Yukon, 1998).

Kwanlin Dün leaders realized that their disputes had a negative effect on how their First Nation was perceived by the federal and territorial governments. Chief Joe Jack in January 1999 observed that the Kwanlin Dün First Nation "can't expect to be taken seriously as a government by other governments if it spends 99 per cent of its time fighting amongst each other" (Tobin, 1999a). A key turning point for the Kwanlin Dün negotiations was the election of Rick O'Brien as chief in March 1999. Under his leadership, the band council's administration of its finances was transparent and the political infighting was subdued to the point that it was no longer reported in the media. O'Brien also re-vived land claims negotiations and established a new negotiating team led by Tom Beaudoin. According to federal and territorial negotiators, bureaucrats, and lawyers, the negotiating team of Tom Beaudoin, Lind-say Staples, Keith Brown, and Mike Smith was highly respected and motivated towards completing a land claims agreement. The combi-nation of the calming effect of Rick O'Brien on Kwanlin Dün politics and the creation of a highly skilled and respected negotiating team did much to change government perceptions of Kwanlin Dün's capacity to negotiate and later on run its own government under a Final Agree-ment (Armour, 2006; Beaudoin, 2006; Brown, 2006; Flynn, 2006; King, 2006; Koepke, 2006; McCullough, 2006; McArthur, 2006).

In terms of possible acculturation effect (that is, those Aboriginal groups that are more Westernized will be more likely to complete a CLC treaty), only a few interviewees mentioned that it mattered. Interviewees did recognize that the Kaska Nations were two of the most traditional Aboriginal groups in the Yukon Territory, with many members continu-ing to speak the Kaska language and regularly going out onto the land for extended periods of time. Kwanlin Dün members, by contrast, were characterized as being more integrated as a result of their history as the Whitehorse Indian Band and as a result of being located in Whitehorse. Furthermore, although elders are extremely important and prominent among the Kaska, they are less so among the Kwanlin Dün. In terms of the effect of acculturation on negotiations, a number of interview-ees mentioned that negotiations in Kaska communities frequently relied on interpreters to communicate information to Kaska members. Others noted that the Kaska are very much wedded to a subsistence economy and have very little understanding of how a modern economy works. In contrast, there was no mention of Kwanlin Dün's need for interpret-ers or about Kwanlin Dün members not understanding how a modern economy works. Despite these observations, it is unclear to what extent acculturation variables affected the Kwanlin Dün and Kaska claims. I would still suggest, however, that acculturation did in some ways con-dition government perceptions of the two Aboriginal groups.

Factors Affecting Speed

Trust Relationships

Trust relationships were present in both sets of negotiations, but in different degrees. For the Kwanlin Dün, the negotiating team prior to Tom Beaudoin had a very negative relationship with federal and territorial officials. Some have described it as 'poisonous,' 'abusive,' and 'mistrustful.' Very little was accomplished because of the posturing and politicking of the Kwanlin Dün team. In contrast, Tom Beaudoin's team was able to create a positive working relationship with government negotiators. All the government officials whom I spoke to mentioned that their relationship with Beaudoin and his team was positive, indicating that trust relationships had been built over the course of negotiations from 1999 to 2005. These trust relationships helped the Kwanlin Dün First Nation quickly complete its treaty in a span of six years.

The Kaska, by contrast, developed a love-hate relationship with government negotiators as a result of the influence of two different Kaska negotiators working on the same team. On the one hand, Kaska chief negotiator Dave Porter was able to build strong working relationships with federal and territorial negotiators. Government negotiators spoke highly of Porter, commending his abilities as a skilled negotiator and strong commitment to negotiating a deal. On the other hand, a number of anonymous interviewees mentioned that a different member of the Kaska negotiating team was a highly negative force with a strong preference towards litigation and highly contentious language and strategies during negotiations. The mention of this individual's name during interviews generally elicited negative reactions regarding his influence among the Kaska. Indeed, even federal, territorial, and Aboriginal interviewees outside of the Kaska process knew of this individual and his reputation for litigation and confrontation. According to one Aboriginal observer, this individual was someone a First Nation should approach only if it wanted to litigate. If a First Nation wanted to negotiate, then it should avoid this person.

Regardless of these dynamics, in both cases trust relationships did have an effect on the speed of negotiations. The Kwanlin Dün team basically started from scratch in 1999 and was able to complete a deal by 2005. One reason why the deal was completed so quickly was the trust relationships built between Kwanlin Dün and government negotiators (Armour, 2006; Beaudoin, 2006; Brown, 2006; Flynn, 2006; Koepke,

2006; McCullough, 2006). For the Kaska, the trust relationship between government negotiators and Dave Porter certainly helped negotiators complete a tentative deal in the summer of 2002. Indeed, this relationship helped cancel out the negative force exerted by one of the members of the Kaska negotiating team. Yet, the Kaska were unable to complete their treaty because they lacked internal cohesion and compatible goals between community-level leaders and members and government officials. The Kaska experience confirms that trust relationships can affect the speed at which a deal is completed, but they do not determine whether a land claims deal will be completed.

Government and External Negotiators

"Government and external negotiator" effects were also not present in the Yukon claims. The federal government did hire an external negotiator, Tim Koepke, for all the Yukon claims. However, by the time he began negotiating with the Kwanlin Dün and the Kaska in the mid-1990s, he was no longer seen as an external negotiator because he had been negotiating for the federal government since the late 1980s. On the territorial side, the negotiators were all career bureaucrats either from within the land claims secretariat or persons transferred to the secretariat from other government departments. Whereas in the Labrador claims particular mention was made of the positive effect of an external negotiator and certain government negotiators on the completion of the Inuit treaty, none of the Yukon Aboriginal interviewees made any special mention of government officials except to say that, for the most part, government negotiators competently represented their governments' interests during negotiations.

Competition for Use of Claimed Lands and Development Pressure

In chapter 2, I discussed Michael Whittington's argument that the first four Yukon claims were completed in 1995 partly because they were located in relatively remote areas of the territory and thus were subject to low land-use competition. The level of land-use competition also had an effect on the speed of negotiations for the Kwanlin Dün and the Kaska. For the Kwanlin Dün, the key complicating factor was that its claim involved lands located within the city of Whitehorse. Territorial officials mentioned that this was one of the main reasons why Kwanlin Dün's negotiations were left to the end (Armour, 2006; Flynn, 2006;

McCullough, 2006). Once negotiations began, land selection, land use planning, and taxation negotiations were all very difficult (Armour, 2006; Beaudoin, 2006; Brown, 2006; Flynn, 2006; McCullough, 2006).

In terms of the Kaska, their traditional lands encompass some of the most mineral-rich and thickly forested areas in the Yukon and most of these resource-rich areas have been licensed to third-party interests. However, the key land issue complicating their negotiations is the transboundary issue. Not only do they claim approximately 25 per cent of the Yukon Territory, but they also claim about 10 per cent of northern British Columbia. Moreover, the Kaska now claim to be "one Kaska Nation" with member groups residing in the Yukon Territory and in northern British Columbia. These competition dynamics make it more likely that their claims will take longer to complete than others elsewhere.

Yet it was partly development pressures that accelerated both claims in the late 1990s. For the Kwanlin Dün, the city's acquisition of the Motorways waterfront property in the late 1990s and its desire to see those lands developed helped facilitate the transfer of those lands to the Kwanlin Dün to complete the treaty. At the time, city officials were in the midst of creating an economic revitalization plan that centred on revitalizing the waterfront to attract tourism. The Kwanlin Dün First Nation was a potential obstacle to that plan, but also a potential facilitator depending on its plans for the lands. According to Mayor Ernie Bourassa (2006), the Kwanlin Dün First Nation ended up being an ideal developer for the city's waterfront lands, since Kwanlin Dün's plan involved building a commercial office building, a retail building, a restaurant, a small hotel, and a cultural centre on the Motorways property.

The deadline imposed by INAC minister Nault was also the result of development pressures. As previously mentioned, negotiations in the Yukon had been the longest outstanding set of negotiations in Canada, dating back to the early 1970s. With most of the claims in the Yukon completed, and with most of the valuable natural resources located in Kaska lands, the deadline was a tool to facilitate development on those lands. The Kaska and the governments had negotiated a freeze on development on Kaska lands that was supposed to last only as long as negotiations. Some interviewees suggested that the deadline was a tool to expedite development, regardless of the outcome: completed treaties would facilitate development by defining what the Kaska had jurisdiction over, but failed treaty negotiations would also facilitate development since the agreement to freeze development on Kaska lands would expire.

Conclusion

This chapter confirms that the four factors specified in chapter 2 also explain the divergent outcomes that the Kwanlin Dün and the Kaska Nations experienced. Specifically, compatible government-Aboriginal goals, choice of Aboriginal tactics, Aboriginal group cohesion as it relates to treaty negotiations, and government perceptions of the Aboriginal group were all important factors in determining completion and non-completion. Also, much as with the Labrador groups, the ability of the Yukon groups to adopt the necessary goals and strategies to complete treaties was conditioned by their historical interactions with the Canadian state and particular attributes of their Aboriginal cultures. For instance, government efforts to relocate and amalgamate the Kwanlin Dün First Nation with the Ta'an Kwäch'än First Nation and with the "come from aways" in Whitehorse made it difficult for the Kwanlin Dün to forge internal cohesion as it related to treaty negotiations and to foster positive government perceptions. This incident is similar to what happened to the Innu, who were forcibly relocated and settled in the twentieth century, with significant negative consequences on internal cohesion and government perceptions of the group. In terms of cultural effects, the Kwanlin Dün was less traditional and more integrated into Western society than the Kaska, which in turn affected the ability of the groups to adopt compatible goals and foster positive government perceptions of the Aboriginal groups. The same, perhaps, can be said about the Inuit and the Innu, with the former more acculturated into Western society than the latter.

The Yukon chapter is also notable for drawing attention to the role that Aboriginal leaders can play in mitigating the effects of conditioning influences. By all accounts, the situation of the KDFN during the 1990s did not leave commentators optimistic about the chances of the First Nation completing a treaty. However, broad leadership changes allowed the group to eliminate its use of confrontational tactics, to forge Aboriginal group cohesion as it related to treaty negotiations, and to foster positive government perceptions of the group. The lesson here is that Aboriginal leaders can act as an effective tool of agency for those Aboriginal groups struggling to complete modern treaty negotiations.

In the next chapter, I discuss the implications of my findings for those groups currently in the treaty process and list a number of alternatives that Aboriginal groups can consider should they no longer be interested in the treaty process.

Chapter Four

Where Do We Go from Here? Options and Alternatives

Rather than being a normative critique of the modern treaty process, the main goal of this book was to generate a social scientific explanation of modern treaty settlements versus non-settlements in Canada. Based on the experiences of four Aboriginal groups in the Yukon Territory and in Labrador, I argue that an Aboriginal group is more likely to complete a comprehensive land claims agreement in the presence of four factors (compatible goals with governments, minimal confrontational tactics, Aboriginal group cohesion as it relates to treaty negotiations, and positive government perceptions of the Aboriginal group). In contrast, a different combination of strategies (incompatible goals, a history of confrontational tactics, Aboriginal group division, and negative government perceptions of the Aboriginal group) will likely prevent an Aboriginal group from completing a modern treaty. The ability of Aboriginal groups to attain either set of factors is conditioned by history, culture, and their interactions with the Canadian state. Yet Aboriginal groups can circumvent some of these conditioning influences through the actions of their leaders.

Although these findings were derived mainly from the experiences of four Aboriginal groups in Labrador and the Yukon Territory, they show significant promise for explaining other settlements and non-settlements in Canada. For instance, Terry Fenge and Paul Quassa (2009), key members of the Inuit negotiating team that negotiated the Nunavut land claims agreement, recently published an article arguing that a number of factors were crucial to their group's success at completing a modern treaty:

- Inuit politicians and negotiators were consistent in their vision for the future and displayed patience and tenacity in their demands to achieve this future. [Aboriginal group cohesion]
- Inuit politicians representing the three regions of Nunavut ... remained united throughout the negotiations, including when there were tensions and uncertainty over drawing the boundary to separate the Inuit and Dene land claims settlement areas that could have resulted in the regions being split into sub-Nunavut, regional settlements. [Aboriginal group cohesion]
- There were close and cooperative relations between staff, many of whom were kabloona (white), and Inuit politicians and negotiators. [Aboriginal group cohesion]
- The parties were willing to compromise on issues the Government of Canada considered to be matters of principle, such as the Crown retaining title to most of the subsurface, and the boundary separating the Inuit and Dene land claims settlement areas. [compatible goals]
- A forward-looking and practical approach was adopted that aimed to avoid embarrassing the Government of Canada. [minimal use of confrontational tactics]
- The focus was concentrated on the Nunavut project throughout the establishment of TFN [Tungavik Federation of Nunavut], whose mandate and sole purpose was to negotiate an agreement with the Government of Canada. [Aboriginal group cohesion] (Fenge and Quassa, 2009: 82–3)

In short, the framework and findings generated here have significant potential for explaining other modern treaty negotiation cases across Canada.

So what are the implications of my findings for Aboriginal groups interested in completing a treaty? Assuming major institutional changes to the treaty process are not forthcoming (see Alcantara, 2009), Aboriginal groups currently in the treaty process face three paths from which they may choose. The first is to complete the treaty process by adopting the strategies discussed in this book. The second is to consider recent initiatives generated within the BC treaty process as a way of jump-starting negotiations. The third is for groups to exit the process and make use of existing legislative and non-legislative mechanisms for increasing governance and negotiating capacity, or to partially reap some of the benefits that a treaty might have provided. Each of these options is discussed below.

Continuing to Negotiate

Assuming the institutional framework remains unchanged, what do these findings mean for practitioners interested in completing treaties? First, Aboriginal groups must be willing and able to accept treaty provisions that are compatible with the goals of the federal, provincial, and territorial governments. In particular, Aboriginal groups, like the KDFN and the Labrador Inuit, must accept some version of the "cede, release, and surrender" provision. Other issues may also be important, such as land selection, land use planning, and the like, but in the four cases studied in this project, the key determinative factor was the willingness of Aboriginal groups to move towards the Crown's position on certainty and finality. Some might argue that the Labrador Inuit did not adopt compatible goals with the government actors because they were able to generate a unique certainty provision: cede, release, but not surrender. Recent research, however, suggests that these supposedly "unique" provisions may not be substantively different from previous certainty provisions found in other modern treaties (Alcantara, 2009). Commenting on the Nisga'a and Tlicho certainty provisions, Peter Kulchyski, for example, writes: "Leave it to the State to find a way to replace one of its oldest, most outdated, ineffective, and unjust policies – the extinguishment clause – with something worse" (Kulchyski, 2005: 100). Martin Papillon suggests that despite the emergence of different certainty formulas, they all lead to the same outcome: "land transactions to ensure legal certainty and facilitate economic development" (Papillon, 2008: 7). These views are shared by a variety of other scholars (Dacks, 2002: 243; Rynard, 2000: 217–21; Blackburn, 2005) and the former federal negotiator for the Nisga'a treaty, Tom Molloy (2000: 110), who wrote that the Nisga'a treaty "provides the same level of certainty as the surrender clauses found in other treaties." Accordingly, Aboriginal groups that want to complete treaties will have to modify their goals as they relate to certainty so that they are compatible with those of governments. Failure to do so will result in non-settlements.

Second, government actors generally react negatively to confrontational tactics because such tactics tend to embarrass them and their governments. Specifically, actions like protests and litigation can generate significant negative publicity for government reputations, especially during election times. Aboriginal groups, like the KDFN and the Inuit, that minimize their use of confrontational tactics and focus on negotiating are more likely to complete treaties. It may be true that the strategic use of these tactics can be useful for breaking negotiating impasses or bringing government actors back to the table, but in the case of the four Aboriginal groups in this study, the frequent use of such tactics was an impediment to negotiations. Therefore, those Aboriginal groups that want to complete treaties and have a history of using confrontational tactics will have to abandon them in favour of focusing solely on negotiating.

Third, Aboriginal groups need to minimize internal group divisions so that they do not distract leaders and negotiators from completing treaty negotiations. One way to mitigate internal divisions is to elect a charismatic and unifying leader. Chief Rick O'Brien of the Kwanlin Dün First Nation was able to heal the wounds caused by the divisive leadership battles that had plagued this First Nation throughout the 1990s. His election as chief of Kwanlin Dün in 1999 was a key factor in paving the way for Kwanlin Dün leaders and negotiators to complete their treaty. The Labrador Inuit had a succession of leaders, board members, and negotiators who were unified in purpose and were able to mitigate any possible problems that might stem from political or community division over the treaty process.

Although possibly problematic for those groups that place great value on collective processes and values, another way to mitigate the problems caused by internal divisions is to minimize the use of community consultations during negotiations, and to maximize their use during a prolonged ratification process. This recommendation is derived from the experiences of the Kwanlin Dün First Nation. In 1999, Kwanlin Dün officials asked government negotiators if negotiations could be held in government offices in downtown Whitehorse. Doing so, they argued, would minimize community disruptions and distractions and allow the negotiators to focus on completing a deal. KDFN officials did undertake some community consultations, such as community meetings and a community advisory council that worked directly with the negotiating team, but these efforts were used relatively sparingly. Once KDFN negotiations were completed, KDFN leaders and negotiators undertook a prolonged ratification process and an intensive informational campaign to convince their members to vote for the treaty.[1] They adopted this ratification strategy based on the experiences of their neighbours, the Carcross/Tagish First Nation. In 2003, they were told that Carcross/Tagish leaders had initially failed to ratify their final agreement because their members had little knowledge about what the treaty entailed and did not have enough time to learn about it.

The one caveat to this strategy is that its effects are unknown post-treaty. It may be that limited consultations lead to higher levels of distrust and conflict during the treaty implementation phase, but the literature and empirical evidence is silent on this issue. Future research is needed to address this question.

Another way of addressing internal division problems is to strengthen the links between Aboriginal negotiators and Aboriginal local leaders. Kaska officials, for instance, were unable to complete their treaty because Kaska Tribal Council leaders and negotiators were disconnected from Ross River Dena Council and Liard First Nation local leaders. Kwanlin Dün officials, by contrast, were more successful in creating cohesive links between their negotiating team, land claims department, and chief and council, and subsequently were able to complete their treaty. Similarly, Labrador Inuit Association (LIA) officials were able to complete their treaty because they established strong links between their community leaders, LIA leaders, and negotiators. Innu officials, however, did not complete their treaty in part because they were distracted by highly divisive relationships between their leaders, negotiators, and members from their two communities.

Finally, Aboriginal groups wanting to complete treaties will have to foster positive government perceptions of their Aboriginal groups. If government officials have poor perceptions of an Aboriginal group, then it is highly unlikely that these officials will be willing to complete a treaty with that group. The task of Aboriginal leaders and negotiators, therefore, is to alter how government officials perceive their groups. Aboriginal groups can demonstrate competency by creating a strong record of financial management and accountability. They can show capacity by successfully assuming control over the provision of certain government programs and services. Finally, they can elect leaders and appoint Aboriginal and non-Aboriginal negotiators who are highly skilled and respected by government officials.

In the next section, I discuss a new treaty-related process that the BC government has introduced to speed up the treaty process. This process is described and analysed in light of the factors described above that produce treaty settlements in Canada.

Incremental Treaty Agreements in British Columbia: A Viable Within-Treaty Process Option?[2]

Over the last several years, the Crown has been heavily criticized for the lack of progress at the negotiating tables, especially in British Columbia (Abele and Prince, 2003; Costa, 2003; Penikett, 2006 [book]; Widdowson and Howard, 2008: 84). In response, the provincial government of British Columbia approached a small number of First Nations about the possibility of signing incremental treaty agreements (ITAs). An incremental treaty agreement is not, nor does it replace, a modern treaty. Instead, an ITA provides a First Nation and the province with treaty-related benefits before completing a treaty. According to the BC government website on ITAs: "Incremental treaty agreements allow First Nations and the Province to enjoy shared benefits in advance of a Final Agreement. Incremental Treaty Agreements build trust among the parties, create incentives to reach further milestones and provide increased certainty over land and resources" (Ministry of Aboriginal Relations and Reconciliation, 2010). ITAs are negotiated between the First Nation and the provincial government. There is no formal federal involvement nor are they a signatory.

The first incremental treaty agreement signed in Canada involved the Tla-o-qui-aht First Nations, an Aboriginal group located next to Tofino, British Columbia. Originally, the Tla-o-qui-aht First Nations were part of the Nuu-chah-nulth Tribal Council, which had entered the British Columbia Treaty Commission process in 1994. In July 2008, however, the Tla-o-qui-aht First Nations left the Tribal Council table due to the lack of progress. To jump-start negotiations, the provincial and Aboriginal negotiators agreed to explore the idea of an incremental treaty agreement that would provide economic certainty, capacity building for the First Nations, and incentives for both parties to complete a treaty. On 13 November 2008, the BC provincial government and the Tla-o-qui-aht First Nations announced the signing of the first-ever ITA in Canada. According to Premier Campbell, "By providing an opportunity to benefit earlier in the treaty process, this agreement helps build trust, creates incentives to reach further milestones, and provides increased certainty over land and resources for the benefit of all British Columbians." Echoing these sentiments, Chief Frances Frank remarked, "Although this is not a final treaty, it is one step towards our ultimate goal of self-determination. Our community believes that creating opportunities today will greatly assist our Nation as we plan for the future" (Office of the Premier, 2008). Under the terms of the four-year agreement, the Tla-o-qui-aht First Nations could receive up to 63 hectares of land and capacity-building funding of up to $600,000. Land and money are released to the First Nations as certain negotiation milestones are completed. For instance:

- On signing the ITA, the First Nations are to receive Lot 124 (16.3 hectares) and $100,000 for capacity building.
- On completing land selection negotiations for the AIP, they are to receive $150,000.
- On signing an AIP, the province agrees to transfer Lot 121 (16.2 hectares).
- The First Nations are to receive $150,000 and $200,000 on the first- and second-year anniversaries of the signing of the land selection portions of the AIP.
- Once a final agreement is initialled, the eastern portion of Lot 120 (12.1 hectares) is to be transferred to the First Nations.
- Upon signing a final agreement, the western portion of Lot 120 (16.5 hectares) and Lot 128 (2 hectares) are to be transferred to the First Nations.

The second incremental treaty agreement in Canada was completed four months later, on 5 March 2009, by the province of British Columbia and the Klahoose First Nation. In the press release announcing the completion of the agreement, BC Minister of Aboriginal Relations and Reconciliation Michael de Jong observed: "The Klahoose Nation is actively pursuing business opportunities to benefit their community. This agreement supports that by allowing the benefits of a treaty to flow to the First Nation earlier in the process. There's no question in the government's mind that ITAs provide a key tool in reconciliation opportunities for First Nations in the shorter term while laying the foundation for a treaty." According to Klahoose First Nation Chief Ken Brown, "We now have closure on an issue that was not only creating difficulty for the Klahoose First Nation, but the government as well" (Ministry of Aboriginal Relations and Reconciliation, 2009). Under the terms of the Klahoose ITA, the First Nation receives $2.1 million to purchase tree licence TFL 10, which has long been held by non-Aboriginal logging companies to extract wood from Klahoose First Nation land. In addition, upon completing the ITA, the First Nation will receive $75,000 and an additional $75,000 within three months of negotiating a tripartite work plan for restarting treaty negotiations towards completing an AIP.

At first glance, ITAs seem to be a positive development for Aboriginal groups currently negotiating treaties. An ITA provides immediate benefits to the First Nations such as ownership rights over key parcels of land as well as funds to help pay for negotiating costs and capacity building. First Nations can also negotiate additional ITAs for other issues to reap the immediate benefits of a treaty and make progress in their treaty negotiations. The Tla-o-qui-aht, for instance, are currently negotiating an ITA with the province to take control over child welfare and other social services. ITAs also provide incentives to the negotiators to complete an AIP and a final agreement, since the benefits of a modern treaty are tied to reaching negotiation milestones like land selection, an initialled AIP, or a tripartite work plan to jump-start negotiations. Indeed, according to government officials, numerous First Nations in British Columbia have approached the province about negotiating ITAs to achieve exactly these results.

ITAs, however, are not without their potential problems. For one, any benefits gained from ITAs are subtracted from what First Nations receive in a final treaty. These benefits are basically treaty-related advances. Second, ITAs, so far, have not had a dramatic effect on the pace or feasibility of completing an AIP and final agreement. According to government and Aboriginal negotiators, few of the milestones in the first two ITAs have been achieved, mainly because the federal government was not involved in the original ITAs. Instead, the federal government has insisted on negotiating its own ITA-like "treaty related measures" with the First Nations before proceeding to AIP negotiations. As well, the contents of the ITAs seem to provide little incentive for the provincial negotiators to complete a treaty. Indeed, it seems that ITAs encourage Aboriginal negotiators to complete treaty negotiations because achieving milestones results in land and monetary benefits for the First Nation. However, ITAs do not seem to have any special or additional effect on the propensity of provincial negotiators to complete a treaty. In comparison to the regular treaty process, the tangible benefits from achieving the milestones set out in an ITA, for the most part, flow solely to the First Nations and not to the Crown. The Crown does gain somewhat, because ITAs potentially facilitate economic development on lands that may or may not have been productive before the completion of an ITA. The province, for instance, hopes that the Tla-o-qui-aht will use their lands to engage in a number of economic development projects. For the Klahoose, however, tree farming and harvesting were already occurring on their lands before their ITA. Now, under their ITA, the Klahoose have simply taken control over the farming and harvesting of forestry resources on their reserve.

Other benefits cited by provincial officials include better relationships with First Nations, creating more support for the treaty process among First Nation governments and community members, and closing the socio-economic gap between Aboriginal and non-Aboriginal citizens in the province. The evidence from Aboriginal and government officials for these claims, however, is mixed. For those First Nations that have completed ITAs, it is unclear whether politicians and citizens are more supportive as a result of signing an ITA. As mentioned above, the Tla-o-qui-aht negotiations have moved slowly and the Klahoose First Nation has yet to complete a tripartite plan. Other First Nations, such as the Haisla, tried to negotiate an ITA but failed to complete one, leading observers to suggest that community members are even more soured on the treaty process as a result of the ITA experience. With regard to the socio-economic impact, the ITAs have not been in place long enough to judge their effects.

More important, ITAs may not be a viable option for some First Nations currently without a modern treaty because it seems that the factors that underlie why some Aboriginal groups can complete CLC agreements may also underlie why some FNs are chosen and able to complete ITAs. Government officials involved in ITAs all mentioned that potential First Nation ITA partners are chosen based on which groups have sound plans to undertake economic development opportunities on their claimed lands. They are also chosen based on the government's assessment of the ability of the groups to "get to the finish line" in modern treaty negotiations. In particular, groups that can demonstrate credible and committed leadership as well as strong community support for a modern treaty are those that are most likely to be chosen to negotiate an ITA.

In short, the ability to complete an ITA may be related to the same factors that produce modern treaty settlements: compatible vs. incompatible goals, minimal vs. extensive use of confrontational tactics, differing levels of Aboriginal group cohesion relating to the treaty process, and positive vs. negative government perceptions of the Aboriginal group. One First Nation in British Columbia failed to complete an ITA because their community leaders and members were divided over what an ITA and a final treaty should provide to the community. Another First

Nation on Vancouver Island saw its ITA negotiations end because it sued the provincial government on an issue unrelated to its ITA. The provincial government ended the negotiations because it refuses to negotiate with an Aboriginal group that engages in litigation with it. Another First Nation that is located near the city of Prince George could not complete its ITA mainly because there were many different families with competing interests that made it impossible for the parties to reach a deal. In contrast, government officials suggest that the two First Nations that did complete ITAs were successful because they had compatible goals, made minimal use of confrontational tactics, had Aboriginal group cohesion relating to the treaty process, and were viewed positively by government officials. Thus, incremental treaty agreements may only be helpful for those groups that are already likely to complete treaty negotiations. However, they may not be helpful to groups like the Innu in Labrador and the Kaska Nations in the Yukon.

Exiting the Treaty Process

If Aboriginal groups are uninterested in continuing with the treaty process or do not want to pursue within-treaty process alternatives like incremental treaty agreements, what alternatives are available? The rest of this chapter discusses three non-treaty alternatives within the existing Canadian legal system that Aboriginal groups might use to pursue their preferences.

Self-Government Agreements

Strictly speaking, comprehensive land claims agreements are usually and can be completely separate from self-government agreements. When Kwanlin Dün leaders and negotiators completed their treaty with the federal government in 2005, they in fact signed two separate documents: the Kwanlin Dün First Nation Final Agreement and the Kwanlin Dün First Nation Self-Government Agreement. Although some Aboriginal groups like the Labrador Inuit, the Labrador Innu, the Tlicho, and eleven of the Yukon First Nations negotiated both agreements concurrently, they were not required to do so and could have chosen to negotiate only a self-government agreement or a comprehensive land claims agreement (Coates and Morrison, 2008: 107).

Based on the experiences of the Kwanlin Dün, the Kaska, the Inuit, and the Innu, it is clear that the most difficult and complicated negotiation issues tend to be those that relate to comprehensive land claims agreements. For instance, the major issues for the four Aboriginal groups studied in this book were land quantum, the "cede, release, and surrender" provision, resource development, hunting and fishing rights, water and waterfront management, taxation of settlement lands, and other related land issues. Self-government issues, while important, tended to be less controversial.

Groups that have become frustrated with comprehensive land claims negotiations might consider focusing their efforts on self-government agreements. These agreements emerged out of the context of the Aboriginal self-government movement in the 1970s and 1980s in response to Aboriginal unhappiness over federal Indian policy. Aboriginal groups at the time were dissatisfied with the long history of ineffective and destabilizing federal interference on their lands and in their lives. As a result, they sought a new model based on substantive Aboriginal self-government for restoring their economies and societies. Federal and provincial officials were initially opposed to their proposal, preferring administrative delegation. According to Coates and Morrison (2008):

> Within a surprisingly short period of time ... the idea of Aboriginal self-government gained political, legal, and constitutional strength. For Aboriginal organizations, self-government emerged as a minimum requirement in their discussions with the Government of Canada. Many Aboriginal politicians, supported by their communities, saw this as the only means of wresting control from the Department of Indian Affairs. For the federal and provincial governments, self-government provided the only widely-supported alternative to an admittedly flawed and unsuccessful system of Aboriginal administration. Even most of those who questioned the utility of empowering small and unprepared Aboriginal governments could not come up with another viable and saleable model for changing the way Canada manages Aboriginal affairs. (106)

As a result, Aboriginal self-government has become a permanent feature of the Aboriginal policy landscape and many groups have or are pursuing self-government through this policy (Belanger and Newhouse, 2008).

The range of self-government models available is both narrow and wide (Alcantara and Whitfield 2010; Chartrand, 2008; Henderson, 2008; Innes and Pelletier, 2008). As with comprehensive land claims negotiations, the federal government prefers to minimize the differences between the multiple treaties it signs with Aboriginal groups while recognizing that the final agreements must be flexible enough to recognize some of the differences between Aboriginal groups. The results have been surprisingly diverse. First Nations agreements, for instance, tend to be community-specific, as opposed to the agreements signed in the Northwest Territories and the Yukon territory, where regional accords tend to dominate. Inuit agreements tend to use either public models of self-government, as in the case of the Nunavut, or ethnic models, such as the Nunatsiavut government in Labrador. Although very little activity has occurred in this area, the federal government is also willing to negotiate agreements with Métis groups and with Aboriginal groups that lack a land base. In short, self-government agreements are a viable option for all Aboriginal groups, and history has shown that there is sufficient flexibility within the policy for groups to design an agreement that fits their community's interests.

One advantage of pursuing self-government agreements separate from the treaty process is that it simplifies negotiations, since the Aboriginal group and the federal government are the only signatory parties to these agreements.[3] One less actor decreases the complexities that come from the involvement of an additional sub-national government. Second, these agreements allow Aboriginal groups to replace the band council structures that were imposed on them by the Indian Act with institutions that are specifically designed to meet their political, cultural, social, and economic needs. At Kwanlin Dün, for instance, the old band council structures have been replaced with a Chief and Council supported by the Elders Council, the Youth Council, the General Assembly, and the Judicial Council (Kwanlin Dün First Nation Self-Government Agreement, 2004; Kwanlin Dün First Nation, n.d.). Third, self-government agreements provide Aboriginal groups with a variety of important and useful powers. For instance, the Kwanlin Dün's self-government agreement recognizes the First Nation as a legal entity for the purposes of borrowing, lending, and transacting. The new Kwanlin Dün government can pass laws affecting language, culture, health care, training, adoption, education, inheritance and wills, solemnization of marriage, administration of its lands, administration of justice, and taxation of its citizens, among other things. For those Aboriginal groups that do not sign a comprehensive land claims agreement, these powers are only applicable to the lands that they control under the Indian Act.

Moreover, such lands remain reserve lands rather than treaty Settlement Lands or Fee Simple Lands. Nonetheless, these powers are more
extensive and are a clear improvement on the powers available to Aboriginal groups under the Indian Act.

One example of a First Nation that signed a self-government agreement before a comprehensive land claims agreement was Westbank
First Nation, located near Kelowna, British Columbia. Westbank First
Nation entered into the British Columbia Treaty Commission process in
1994, completing a Framework Agreement in 1997. Since then, however,
the First Nation has made little progress in negotiating an agreement-
in-principle with the federal and provincial governments. According to
Tim Raybould, Westbank's chief negotiator:

> Treaty negotiations have not been "negotiations" for many years. Gov-
> ernments come to the table with poorly thought out take-it-or-leave-it
> positions that serve neither the province nor Canada well, nor, indeed,
> first nations. Treaties have become way too complicated. They are not de-
> signed to be living documents but rather "full and final settlements," a
> dangerous approach that may result in future conflict. If B.C. and Canada
> truly want economic certainty, they had better realize who actually needs
> the treaties. (Raybould, 2007)

Negotiations on a self-government agreement, however, have been
much more fruitful. On 6 July 2000, Westbank and federal negotiators initialled the Westbank First Nation Self-Government Agreement.
Westbank community members ratified this agreement on 24 May 2003,
and officials signed it on 3 October 2003. Under the agreement, the First
Nation can create its own governing institutions and has jurisdiction
over a number of important powers. It can and has passed laws governing wills and estates, taxation, management of reserve lands, resource
management, agriculture, environmental protection, culture and language, education, health services, law enforcement, traffic enforcement, public order, and public works, among other things. Indeed, as
a result of its self-government agreement, Westbank First Nation has
been able to construct the most comprehensive and effective system
of laws regulating Aboriginal community lands in Canada (Flanagan,
Alcantara, and Le Dressay, 2010: 156–7). Self-government agreements,
therefore, are powerful instruments for building "tribal sovereignty,"
which a number of scholars have argued is necessary for successful
economic development on Canadian Indian reserves (see, for instance,

Cornell and Kalt, 1992; Alcantara, 2007b; Flanagan, Alcantara, and Le Dressay, 2010).

There are, of course, some criticisms of the self-government agreement policy. Some, for instance, suggest that self-government under the federal policy is actually self-administration (Papillon, 2008). Others suggest that Aboriginal self-government agreements, rather than emancipating Aboriginal peoples from the Canadian system, embed them more firmly within the Canadian constitutional and legal framework. Critics also suggest that some communities are far too small to have meaningful self-government, while others lack the capacity to succeed (Coates and Morrison, 2008: 115–17). Nonetheless, based on the experiences of some Aboriginal groups that have signed self-government agreements (Alcantara and Whitfield, 2010; Flanagan, Alcantara, and Le Dressay, 2010: 152–8; Henderson, 2008; Slowey, 2008), and if viewed as an alternative for those groups that are unable or willing to sign a modern treaty, self-government agreements may be a viable option for some Aboriginal groups.

Bilateral Agreements

A second option that is available to Aboriginal groups is bilateral agreements, also known as accommodation or interim agreements. These documents are used by governments, Aboriginal groups, and third-party interests to seek agreement on particular issues relating to Aboriginal lands. In 2003 the Kaska signed a bilateral agreement with the Yukon Territorial government to co-manage the forest resources on their traditional lands (Bi-Lateral Agreement between the Kaska and the Yukon Government, 2003). The Carrier Sekani First Nations in British Columbia withdrew from the treaty process in March 2007 to pursue bilateral agreements with private companies such as the Canfor Corporation to develop the natural resources on their lands (Brethour, 2007: A2).

Besides the time and monetary advantages that come from negotiating specific agreements between two parties, bilateral agreements give Aboriginal groups a number of other advantages. First, they allow Aboriginal groups to get involved immediately in those lands that are being developed by governments and businesses while treaty negotiations are occurring. According to tribal chief David Luggi, "While they keep us talking at the [comprehensive land claims negotiating] table, resource extraction continues" (Brethour, 2007: A2). By withdrawing from the process and pursuing bilateral agreements, however, Aboriginal groups can gain immediate control over the development of their lands. Private companies will seek bilateral agreements with Aboriginal groups even if they have acquired licences from the provincial government because the *Taku River* and the *Haida* decisions[4] require governments and other interests to consult or accommodate affected First Nations before their lands can be developed.

A second advantage of bilateral agreements is that governments may be willing to be more flexible. For instance, although the Yukon territorial government long opposed the idea of a Kaska veto over all Kaska lands during treaty negotiations, it accepted this veto in a bilateral co-management of forestry resources agreement negotiated outside of the claims process. The preamble of this bilateral agreement states: "WHEREAS: [the] Yukon [territorial government] acknowledges, in agreements entered into with the Kaska in January 1997, that the Kaska have Aboriginal rights, titles, and interest in and to the Kaska Traditional Territory in the Yukon" (Bi-Lateral Agreement between the Kaska and the Yukon Government, 2003: 1). Moreover, under section 3.0, entitled "Kaska Consent," the agreement states that the "Yukon [territorial government] shall not agree to any significant or major dispositions of interests in lands or resources or significant or major authorizations for exploration work and resource development in the Kaska Traditional Territory without consulting and obtaining the consent of the Kaska" (ibid.: 4).

According to a number of interviewees, Yukon territorial officials were willing to accept a Kaska veto in the bilateral agreement because the agreement was not a constitutional treaty. Moreover, the government was strongly interested in developing the rich forest resources on Kaska lands and was cognizant of its duty to consult or accommodate Kaska interests before it could extract those resources. Finally, the bilateral agreement had an expiry date of two years, at which time either party could terminate the agreement with sixty days' notice. Soon after the two years expired, the territorial government terminated the agreement, since it was satisfied with the amount of resources extracted from the affected lands. Kaska officials believe that the rights they gained in the bilateral agreement have set a precedent for all subsequent agreements, including modern treaties, with the territorial government. Territorial officials disagree, however, stating that the expiry of the bilateral agreement means that their government no longer has to recognize a Kaska veto over Kaska traditional lands.

In sum, bilateral agreements show promise, albeit within limits, in giving Aboriginal peoples immediate and significant control over resource developments on their lands. Moreover, bilateral agreement negotiations tend to be quicker, more cost effective, and focused, since the stakes are lower and considerably less complex. Governments, at least in the case of the Kaska, have shown a willingness to be more flexible in recognizing Aboriginal rights and title than they are during comprehensive land claims negotiations. There are, however, several important limitations to bilateral agreements. They tend to be used only for resource development projects and not for other purposes like fishing and hunting rights. Moreover, they tend to last for a specific period of time, meaning that the rights that Aboriginal groups may gain through bilateral agreements may not transfer to future agreements. Nonetheless, although bilateral agreements are not treaty agreements, they are becoming more common in Canada.

First Nations Land Management Act

For those groups reluctant to take on the responsibilities that flow from a self-government agreement, another option is to opt into the First Nations Land Management Act (FNLMA), passed by the federal government in 1999. In the early 1990s, Chiefs Robert Louie (Westbank First Nation), Austin Bear (Muskoday First Nation), and Strater Crowfoot (Siksika First Nation) approached the federal government on behalf of thirteen (later fourteen) First Nations about creating a legislative framework for opting out of the land management provisions of the Indian Act to create their own land codes for managing their reserve lands. The driving forces behind their proposal were twofold. First, they were unhappy with the economic drag that stemmed from their lands remaining under the authority of the Indian Act and, second, they hoped to further their goals of Aboriginal self-government and self-determination by taking control over the management of their reserve lands. The federal government agreed, signing a framework agreement with the fourteen First Nations in February 1996 and then passing enabling legislation in 1999. In essence, the FNLMA allows an Aboriginal group to opt out of the land management provisions of the Indian Act to develop its own land code for managing its reserve lands. To do so requires First Nations to apply to INAC to become signatories to the FNLMA. In 1999, only fourteen First Nations were allowed to participate. Since then, forty-one bands have opted into the FNLMA, ninety have inquired about doing so, and eighteen have had their land codes put into force (Alcantara, 2007b; Flanagan, Alcantara, and Le Dressay, 2010: 108–9).

The FNLMA potentially provides Aboriginal groups who have not completed a modern treaty, like the Labrador Innu, with a number of advantages. First, there is very little negotiating involved. A First Nations voluntarily opts into the legislation to develop and draft a land code, submits it to a jointly appointed verifier, negotiates a funding agreement with Indian and Northern Affairs Canada, and then holds a community vote on both the land code and the funding agreement. Once approved, the verifier certifies the land code and the First Nation takes over all land management responsibilities from the Crown. The average time to complete a land code is 1068 days (Isaac, 2005).

Second, much like self-government agreements, the FNLMA gives signatory First Nations the opportunity to build administrative and governing capacity and to increase tribal sovereignty. The Labrador Innu, for instance, should they opt into the act, could design a land management regime and pass laws according to their local customs and needs. Their land code could address individual property rights, collective property rights, leases and licences, matrimonial property rules, dispute resolution processes involving band lands, and other law-making jurisdictions. Some groups have designed land management regimes that mimic off-reserve regimes, while others have combined the efficiency of off-reserve property rights with rules that allow for the expropriation of individual interests depending on the needs of the community.

Most important, the federal government under the FNLMA no longer has any role in the management of reserve lands nor do they collect any rents or royalties. Previously, for instance, INAC was heavily involved in the approval and management of leases and rents. Now, under the FNLMA, First Nations that develop their own land codes manage and collect leases and rents directly. These monies can then be used to build up administrative and governance capacity relating to land management. In short, the FNLMA encourages capacity building and Indigenous sovereignty and self-government by eliminating the involvement of the federal government and transferring land management responsibilities to the First Nations (Alcantara, 2007b; Alcantara 2008a).

Recent evidence confirms that although First Nations do not receive the same ownership and administrative rights that a treaty would provide, the FNLMA still provides substantial benefits. At Muskoday First Nation, for instance, the band eliminated federal involvement and crafted a land code that better reflected the wishes and desires of their community's elders and members. At Shxwha:y First Nation in British Columbia, observers have commented that "the approval of the Shxwha:y Village's Land Code has proven to be of great benefit to the community ... Shxwha:y Village's first concrete example of this was in their ability to obtain a Timber Mark from the BC Ministry of Forestry. The process took them less than 10 days. With INAC, it took them 6 months" (First Nations Land Advisory Board, 2008: 24). At the Nipissing First Nation in Ontario, the band has also used its land code to greatly improve its investment climate, attracting investors to build a motel, travel agency, storage facility, recreational vehicle sales and servicing facility, coffee shop, convenience store, gas stations, tobacco product manufacturer, and office complex on the reserve (Flanagan, Alcantara, and Le Dressay, 2010: 117–19).

Conclusion

Aboriginal groups that have yet to complete a treaty have a number of options that they can pursue to fulfil their goals as they relate to the Canadian state. Continued participation in the treaty process, as this book has argued, requires Aboriginal groups to find a way to achieve the necessary factors to complete a modern treaty. Incremental treaty agreements may provide a within-process mechanism for jump-starting or facilitating treaty completion. Unfortunately, however, it may be that only those groups that already have the necessary factors to complete a treaty can benefit from ITAs. As well, the model is far too new to make any firm conclusions about its viability as a tool for facilitating treaty completion. Nonetheless, groups that are no longer interested in the treaty process, yet want to accrue some of the benefits that a treaty was supposed to deliver, can access a number of policy alternatives that, although they fall short of the benefits and rights gained under a modern treaty, may still provide useful benefits as a replacement to modern treaties or as a tool to build capacity towards completing a modern treaty.

Conclusion

Comprehensive land claims agreements are fundamentally important and contested tools of public policy. Much of the literature on modern treaties has taken a normative perspective in which value judgments have been assigned to the different processes and outcomes produced. As well, a rich body of scholarship has emerged alongside the normative literature that has examined inductively the evolution of these negotiations into treaty settlements. This book has tried to add to these literatures by taking a different approach to the subject, one that is more explanatory than normative, and one that is more deductive than inductive. At the root of this approach is the assumption that comprehensive land claims negotiations are essentially bargaining situations in which Aboriginal and government participants negotiate to achieve their preferences. By specifying the institutional framework and the preferences and incentives of the players, we can determine precisely which strategies (compatible goals; limited confrontational tactics; internal cohesion; and positive government perceptions) produce settlements and which do not, at least for the four groups that are the focus of this book. The ability to pursue these strategies is affected by historical and cultural legacies that are generally beyond the control of the Indigenous groups. Yet Aboriginal leaders can mitigate these legacies and thus influence the ability of their groups to complete a final agreement. Recent research suggests that these findings are generalizable, and I hope that scholars and practitioners will directly apply them to, and test them against, other cases of comprehensive land claims negotiations in Canada.

Others may wish to use this framework to study other policy areas that involve differential power relationships. The specific claims process, for instance, is another type of bargaining situation involving Crown and Aboriginal actors negotiating settlements that maximize their preferences. The framework developed in this book may give scholars the theoretical tools to understand the relative slowness and unsatisfactory outcomes being produced by that process. Outside of the Aboriginal politics subfield, scholars might draw upon the framework to explain variation in negotiations between two levels of government, where one level of government is a constitutional actor and the other is not. Three sets of intergovernmental relationships in Canada come immediately to mind. The first is negotiations between the federal government and a municipality/regional government. The second is negotiations between a provincial government and a municipality/regional government. The third is the relationship between the federal government and territorial governments. In each case, unequal actors are engaging in intergovernmental bargaining to achieve their preferences within a set of incentivized conditions. This book may provide some useful analytical tools for studying these relationships.

Postscript

Since the completion and submission of this book manuscript to University of Toronto Press for publication, a number of important developments relating to the Labrador Innu have occurred. Originally, the Innu research for this book was undertaken in 2006. Based on that research, I found that for much of their negotiating history, the Innu have not been able to achieve the necessary strategies to complete a treaty. However, I also found that post-2001, there was some evidence that the Labrador Innu were starting to experience some internal changes that would potentially improve their ability to complete a treaty. The results of those changes recently culminated in a series of significant negotiation milestones in 2010 and 2011. On 17 February 2010, Innu Nation leaders and officials from the Government of Newfoundland and Labrador announced the signing of several new agreements that purportedly settled all of the outstanding issues outlined in the Tshash Petapen (New Dawn) Agreement. In particular, these new agreements addressed all provincial-Innu issues relating to the Lower and Upper Churchill developments and contained an agreement-in-principle on the Innu land claim. A year and a half later, the Innu communities of Sheshatshiu and Natuashish held a ratification vote on the New Dawn Agreement and its subsequent agreements. On 4 July 2011, CBC news online reported that 90 per cent of voters in the two Innu communities voted in favour of the New Dawn Agreements. Although official results have not been released, an anonymous provincial government official and several Innu community members indicated to me that approximately 84 per cent of voters in Sheshatshiu and 95 per cent of voters in Natuashish voted in favour of the agreements. As a result, the Labrador Innu have completed an AIP and can now proceed to negotiate a final agreement with the federal and provincial governments.

The signing and ratification of the AIP is a significant milestone for the Labrador Innu, especially in light of the ratification vote results. These events and results suggest that there is some hope that the Labrador Innu will be able to successfully negotiate and ratify a final agreement with the Crown. If they are successful in completing a final agreement, what might explain these new developments? In chapter 2, I highlighted a number of important internal changes that seemed to have moved the Innu in the right direction towards treaty completion. One significant change was the return of Peter Penashue to a position of leadership within Innu Nation. Although the death of Grand Chief Ben Michel in August 2006 was a significant loss to both communities, it did pave the way for Penashue, a long-time supporter of negotiating a treaty within the current process, to return as president of Innu Nation. Indeed, it was under his leadership that the Innu were able to successfully initiate the land claims process in 1991 and complete a Framework Agreement in 1996. Once he returned as president in 2006, Penashue was instrumental in successfully concluding negotiations on the New Dawn Agreement in 2008. Since then, he has been replaced by a set of leaders who are similarly supportive of signing a final agreement. When I originally wrote chapter 2, I mentioned that this change in leadership could have a significant impact on the Innu's land claims negotiations and specifically on the compatibility of Innu and government goals. Although the AIP is not yet publicly available, an analysis of the New Dawn Agreement in chapter 2 and the events described above suggest that this is what may have happened.

In addition to these important changes, the Innu have also experienced change with respect to the other factors that affect land claims negotiations. They have, for instance, avoided the use of litigation, protests, and other forms of contentious politics throughout the 2000s (Alcantara, 2010), thus satisfying another criterion for treaty completion. They have also fostered positive government perceptions by focusing on community development, healing, and capacity building through "The Labrador Innu Comprehensive Healing Strategy," as suggested by federal officials and community members in the early 2000s. The Innu communities also pursued and completed registration and band creation under the Indian Act, achieving band status in 2002 and receiving reserve lands in 2006. These efforts have not only had a positive effect on the federal and provincial governments' perceptions of the

Innu, but also on the community and its ability to focus attention on supporting a land claims agreement. In short, over the last ten years, the Innu have slowly worked towards achieving the necessary strategies for completing a treaty.

Despite these positive events, a number of significant obstacles remain. The most important one is the certainty and finality provision, which was left undefined in the recently ratified AIP and must now be negotiated during final agreement negotiations. The willingness of the Innu to accept a provision that is consistent with the certainty models agreed to by other Aboriginal groups in Canada will be crucial for determining the final outcome (Alcantara, 2009). Whether the Innu will be able to overcome this obstacle will depend partly on the commitment of their leaders to completing a treaty and the ability of those leaders to successfully manage the community ratification process once a final agreement is reached.

Notes

Introduction

1 Christa Scholtz (2006) suggests that the federal government adopted a treaty negotiation policy not because of the *Calder* decision per se, but because Aboriginal peoples organized and mobilized effectively during the 1960s and 1970s. In essence, negotiation policies emerge only when significant Aboriginal mobilization occurs *before* positive judicial decisions.
2 The first six groups were the James Bay Cree, the Inuvialuit in the western part of the Northwest Territories, the Nisga'a in British Columbia, the Council of Yukon Indians in the Yukon Territory, the Inuit in the eastern Northwest Territories, and the Dene and Métis in the Northwest Territories.
3 In addition to comprehensive land claims negotiations, the Canadian state has created the specific claims process to address alleged wrongs or mistakes committed by the federal government in its interpretation and implementation of Aboriginal treaties. The process can also be used by non-treaty Aboriginal groups to address the federal government's mismanagement of Indian assets. For instance, the Blood Tribe in Alberta is negotiating with the federal government through the specific claims process for unpaid compensation for lands surrendered to the Crown in 1889. The Mississaugas in Ontario are negotiating with the federal government over the alleged invalid surrender of 200 hectares of land on the north shore of the Credit River in 1820 (Specific Claims Branch of Indian and Northern Affairs Canada, 2006: 2, 65). Although the specific claims process is an important part of the evolving treaty relationship between Aboriginal

and non-Aboriginal peoples, this book focuses on comprehensive land claims agreements because of their significant scope and nature.

4 See J.R. Miller's (2000) discussion of directed versus non-directed change regarding Indian–White relations in Canada.

5 On the rationality of government actors involved in Aboriginal policy, see Irlabacher-Fox, 2009. On the rationality of Indigenous actors, see Alfred (2008, 17), who quotes John Mohawk, "a respected and influential Rotinohshonni historian" as saying, "All human beings possess the power of rational thought; all human beings can think; all human beings have the same kind of needs; all human beings want what is good for society; all human beings want peace ... Out of that idea will come the power ... that will make the people of the [Rotinohshonni] among the most influential thinkers in the history of human thought ... The basic fundamental truth contained in that idea is that so long as we believe that everybody in the world has the power to think rationally, we can negotiate them to a position of peace."

6 Following the tradition of other rational choice approaches (for instance, see Kam, 2000; Simeon, 2006), I treat government and Aboriginal governments/organizations as unitary actors when specifying their preferences and incentives to negotiate. Interview data and documents cited later in the book support this assumption.

7 A normative analysis would focus on such questions as, To what extent does the treaty process produce just outcomes? Is the treaty process fair and equitable? In contrast, this book takes an explanatory approach by identifying factors that determine variation in modern treaty settlements versus non-settlements. It does not attempt to apply value judgments to the phenomena, actors, and processes under examination.

1. Setting the Stage: The Context of Modern Treaty Negotiations in Canada

1 A complete and comprehensive history of treaty making in Canada is beyond the scope of this book. I would refer readers to RCAP (1996) and Miller (2009), the most comprehensive and authoritative histories on this topic.

2 As discussed in the introduction, some suggest that settlements are produced by changes in federal policy. The findings in this book suggest that these types of policy changes affect all Aboriginal groups at the same time, and therefore do not help tease out the factors that explain why some groups complete treaties and others do not.

3 Indeed, an amendment in 1983 to s. 35 removes any doubts about the constitutional status of comprehensive land claims agreements in Canada.

4 Although the territories have developed into quasi-provinces, they still do not have the same level of control or jurisdiction over their lands that the provinces enjoy. Indeed, even in the case of Yukon, which completed a devolution transfer agreement in 2003 relating to lands and resources, the territorial government has only administrative legislative control rather than constitutional jurisdiction over its lands and resources.

5 These issues are discussed in more detail in the empirical chapters. For now, see Haysom, 1990.

6 This is also probably true because a number of Aboriginal informants mentioned that provincial and territorial officials were more inflexible than federal ones.

7 By contrast, the Northwest Territories has a consensus-style government (White, 2003).

8 Indeed, this decision is consistent with other rational choice approaches in the literature. For example, see Kam, 2000; Simeon, 2006.

9 One might infer from this point that businesses, therefore, have a powerful effect on government positions during negotiations. However, every interviewee I spoke to suggested that business interests had no direct effect on negotiations. Some interviewees suggested that in cases where business interests may have attempted to apply indirect influence to the negotiating table, the effects of such influence were marginal at best.

10 Indeed, Stephanie Irlbacher-Fox (2009) argues in her recent book that even when government officials have the best of intentions, they continue to negotiate as rational actors would, focusing on their own economic and political goals.

11 The parties were free to negotiate a freeze on development for lands up to the specified amount listed in the Umbrella Final Agreement for each Yukon First Nation. The Kaska First Nations, for instance, were able to negotiate an agreement to protect 9450 square kilometres from development until 2008 (see Small, 2002c).

12 As described in the introductory chapter incentives to delay or negotiate are generated by the relevant institutional framework governing comprehensive land claims negotiations in Canada.

13 "Nitassinan" is what the Innu call their traditional lands in Labrador and Quebec.

14 This is not to say that Aboriginal peoples are without sovereignty. In *Campbell v. British Columbia* (2000) BCSC 1123, BC Supreme Court Judge Williamson argued that Aboriginal peoples retain some sovereignty. In paragraph 179, Judge Williamson states: "I have concluded that after the assertion of sovereignty by the British Crown, and continuing to and after

the time of Confederation, although the right of aboriginal people to govern themselves was diminished, it was not extinguished. Any aboriginal right to self-government could be extinguished after Confederation and before 1982 by federal legislation which plainly expressed that intention, or it could be replaced or modified by the negotiation of a treaty. Post-1982, such rights cannot be extinguished, but they may be defined (given content) in a treaty. The Nisga'a Final Agreement does the latter expressly." And in paragraph 181, he states: "Section 35 of the *Constitution Act, 1982*, then, constitutionally guarantees, among other things, the limited form of self-government which remained with the Nisga'a after the assertion of sovereignty. The Nisga'a Final Agreement and the settlement legislation give that limited right definition and content. Any decision or action which results from the exercise of this now-entrenched treaty right is subject to being infringed upon by Parliament and the legislative assembly. This is because the Supreme Court of Canada has determined that both aboriginal and treaty rights guaranteed by s. 35 may be impaired if such interference can be justified and is consistent with the honour of the Crown." Furthermore, in the *Mitchell* decision, although Justice Binnie denies the existence of external sovereignty, he does recognize the internal sovereignty of the Mohawks within the Canadian state.

15 It is unclear whether the provinces are subject to the exact same fiduciary duty as the federal government. The *Haida* case, for instance, mentions that the provincial government has a duty to consult *and* accommodate, but elsewhere says the government has a duty to consult *or* accommodate. Future litigation may clear up whether provincial governments are indeed subject to a fiduciary duty. These issues are discussed in further detail in chapter 4.

16 Some may suggest that courts have not been given enough explanatory weight here for affecting the propensity for negotiations to lead to a settlement. Although judicial decisions do affect the broader institutional framework within which negotiations take place, they do not help explain why some groups have completed treaties and why others have not. In the next chapter, I describe how despite the Innu and the Inuit successfully obtaining a court injunction against Inco, only the Inuit were able to capitalize on the judicial outcome.

17 For details on the relationship between RCAP and *Gathering Strength*, see Abele (1999: 450–3).

18 The key judicial decisions are *Haida Nation v. British Columbia (Minister of Forests)*, 2004 SCC 73 [2004] 3 S.C.R. 511, and *Taku River Tlingit First Nation*

v. British Columbia (Project Assessment Director), 2004 SCC 74, [2004] 3 S.C.R. 550.

19 See also Salée (2006: 25), Dacks (1981: 61, 64), Irlbacher-Fox (2009). This characterization of government reluctance to settle land claims also applies in British Columbia (see for instance Penikett, 2006 [book]). According to BC Auditor General Arn van Iersel and federal Auditor General Sheila Fraser, Premier Gordon Campbell prefers interim agreements over land claim agreements because the latter are too difficult and expensive to negotiate, and have too much potential to adversely affect the powers of the province. Tony Penikett points out that the federal government is also reluctant to quickly complete agreements. This reluctance, he argues, is the result of the influence of federal treasury officials and risk-adverse civil servants who prefer endless negotiations to completed agreements (Cayo, 2006). Indeed, although federal officials constantly proclaim that they want certainty, the evidence seems to suggest that more often than not they benefit from uncertainty as negotiations languish.

2. The Innu and the Inuit in Labrador

1 The large population range is the result of differences in Nunatsiavut and Statistics Canada data collection and classification methods. For instance, the Statistics Canada data do not include *Kablunângajuit*.

2 Innu members refer to this first settlement as "Davis Inlet I."

3 Murray Coolican's report, delivered in 1986, had four central principles. Comprehensive land claims agreements should recognize and affirm Aboriginal rights, allow for the negotiation of more expansive self-government arrangements, lead to the sharing of jurisdiction and management of lands and resources, and ensure the fair treatment of third-party interests. The most important finding of the report was that the federal government's "blanket extinguishment" requirement was a significant obstacle to the completion of comprehensive land claims agreements in Canada. Indeed, one might argue that it is problematic for the fiduciary to adopt a bargaining position in which it demands that the ward extinguish its rights and title (see Graham, 1987; INAC, 2003).

4 "Gathering Strength" refers to the policy created by the federal government in response to the RCAP report. See Abele, 1999: 450–3.

5 Individuals who decided not to vote were counted as voting "no" to ratification. It is also important to note that holding a ratification vote for an AIP was unusual at the time. Today, the federal government insists that

First Nations ratify their AIPs to help pave the way for successful Final Agreement ratification votes.

6 Interviewees were asked whether business interests had any direct or indirect impact on government or Aboriginal negotiators. The overwhelming response from Aboriginal and non-Aboriginal interviewees was that businesses had no direct influence and if they did have an indirect impact, it was relatively small. The pressure for development is incorporated into the argument later on in the matrix of factors affecting speed.

7 The three agreements were an Impact and Benefits Agreement with Inco, an Interim Measures agreement with the federal and provincial government, and an Environmental Management agreement with the two levels of government.

8 This fact was why overall Inuit support was only 76.4% despite the high levels of support reported in the subsequent sentences, which report the results for only those Inuit who voted and do not include the automatic "no" votes from non-voters.

9 Penashue was president until 1997 and then again from 1999–2004 before being defeated in an election by Ben Michel. In August 2006 Michel died of a sudden heart attack and was replaced in the interim by Innu Nation vice-president Daniel Benuen. In September 2006, Daniel Ashini, former Innu Nation land claims negotiator and cousin to Ben Michel, was elected Innu Nation president. Daniel Benuen remains Innu Nation vice-president. Recently, Ashini passed away and Penashue was elected president. He later resigned to run as a Conservative candidate in the 2011 federal election.

10 Unfortunately, I was unable to acquire detailed results.

11 Backhouse and McRae do not indicate why the Innu strategy of demanding the best element of previous treaties was unacceptable to government officials. Based on my research findings, I would speculate that government officials were reluctant because they had negative perceptions of the Innu group. Officials were probably afraid that the Innu did not have the capacity to succeed if they gave the Innu the "best element[s] of every land claim negotiated by Aboriginal peoples across the country." The Innu communities have already generated a lot of negative publicity for both levels of government over the last twenty years and treaty implementation failure would only further harm the reputations of the federal and provincial governments.

12 Both the Innu and the Inuit have formally clarified their interests in the Voisey's Bay area. Inuit interests are codified in their Final Agreement while Innu interests are laid out in a memorandum of agreement

and an impact and benefits agreement with the federal and provincial governments.

13 As will be discussed later, consultation is a strong norm among the Innu. It may be that consultations did not occur before the agreement because of the change in leadership after Ben Michel's death.

14 The first six groups were the James Bay Cree, the Inuvialuit in the Northwest Territories (NWT), the Nisga'a in British Columbia, the Yukon First Nations, the Inuit of Nunavut, and the Dene and Métis in the NWT.

15 In addition to all the Inuit interviewees I spoke with mentioning strong community cohesion, see the interview with the LIA's chief land claims negotiator, Toby Andersen (Nunatsiavut Government, 2005), who says: "One of the things that I remember and appreciate is that we weren't hounded by our own people. They'd say 'you're doing well, continue on.'"

16 I wish to thank one particular anonymous reviewer for helping me to unpack this concept more clearly.

17 For a similar point, see Simeon, 2006: 13.

3. The Kwanlin Dün First Nation and the Kaska Nations in the Yukon Territory

1 Unlike other parts of Canada, there are no Métis groups in the Yukon.

2 The exception is Treaty 8, which included a small portion of Yukon lands in the southeastern part of the territory.

3 See chapter 2, note 3.

4 Some might argue that any framework that attempts to explain factors that affect differences in negotiation speeds must take into account the role of political actors. Although it is true that political actors can speed up or slow down negotiations, their effects in my four cases are universal. For instance, the appointment of Bob Nault and Ron Irwin speeded up negotiations with all Yukon First Nations, but it had little effect on explaining the differences *between* First Nations. Therefore, political actors are not included in the framework.

5 The Northern Native Broadcasting, Yukon (NNBY), provides radio (CHON-FM 98.1) and television (NEDAA) programing on issues affecting Indians living in the Yukon. The NNBY is owned and operated by the fourteen Yukon First Nations.

6 To clarify, Kwanlin Dün members who lived on off-reserve lands were subject to taxation and had income tax deducted from non-Kwanlin Dün First Nation employers at source.

7 According to several Kaska interviewees, KTC negotiators were very much enamoured with the "rich" lifestyle involved in comprehensive land claims negotiations. This included expensive meals and staying at fancy hotels.

8 For a discussion of sunk costs and lock-in effects, see Knill and Lenschow (2001: 201).

9 Even in death, Elijah Smith remains a respected and influential figure among Yukon First Nations. Indeed, one Liard First Nation elder, who is a staunch opponent of land claims, says that if Elijah Smith were alive today, the Kaska would have probably signed a final agreement by now.

10 The exceptions to this rule are Dave Porter, Kaska chief negotiator, and, to a lesser extent, Hammond Dick, Kaska tribal leader chief. Indeed, observers from all three parties have mentioned that Porter is very much interested in negotiating a deal through the Umbrella Agreement. However, the rest of the Kaska leadership and band members are much more reluctant and are suspicious of the Umbrella Agreement.

11 According to one anonymous source, the federal government may have known that the ratification process was not undertaken correctly. The evidence for this is a memo that the source thinks informs federal government officials that the UFA ratification was not done properly. This memo apparently was filed by a government lawyer before the passage of the federal legislation enacting the Umbrella Agreement in 1994.

12 The following is a list of Kaska litigation against the federal, provincial, and territorial governments regarding their land claims (with the current status of each court case as of November 2006 in parentheses): (1) *Stone et al. v. Her Majesty the Queen* ("HMQ"), Federal Court no. T-2828-86 (in abeyance since the fall of 2003); (2) *Kaska Dena Council* ("KDC") *v. HMQ*, FC no. T-1209-99 (in abeyance since the fall of 2003); (3) *Ross River Dena Council* ("RRDC") *and Liard First Nation v. HMQ*, FC no. T-1749-99 (ongoing); (4) *KDC v. HMQ*, FC no. T-138-01 (in abeyance since the fall of 2003); (5) *KDC v. British Columbia*, BCSC no. L043150 (awaiting judgment); (6) *RRDC v. HMQ*, Supreme Court of Yukon ("SCY") no. 05-A0043 (ongoing); (7) *KDC v. HMQ*, BCSC no. S-061757 (ongoing); (8) *RRDC v. HMQ*, SCY no. 06-A009 (ongoing).

13 The one potential drawback of this strategy post-treaty is that it might create a significant amount of distrust and alienation towards the new Aboriginal government. However, there is nothing to indicate that these issues have occurred within the KDFN post-treaty.

14 To clarify, an Aboriginal person can be a beneficiary of one First Nation, and a member of another. In practical terms, only beneficiaries can vote on and benefit from a CLC agreement.

15 I think that the Kaska, especially those in Ross River, are also struggling with more severe economic and social problems because of the mine in nearby Faro, which opened during the 1960s. This mine brought the Kaska in Ross River into sustained contact with non-Aboriginal peoples for the first time and introduced a permanent and easily accessible supply of alcohol and drugs to the community. Compared to Liard First Nation, Ross River is clearly having a harder time with social and economic problems stemming mainly from significant alcohol and drug abuse. These socioeconomic problems, therefore, are partly the result of state development and interference effects.

16 Some might wonder how Porter and Dick continue in their leadership roles if they are out of step with their communities on the issue of land claims negotiations. A number of anonymous interviewees suggest that Porter's support comes from those few members who want a treaty settlement. He also comes from a well-respected Kaska family and has built a reputation as an important spokesperson for the Kaska Nation. Hammond Dick's support comes from his long-standing appointment as the first and only tribal chief of the Kaska Tribal Council. It bears noting as well that he was not elected through popular vote. Rather, his lifetime appointment was the result of a decision by the KTC's board of directors.

4. Where Do We Go from Here? Options and Alternatives

1 Peter Kulchyski (2005: 252) quotes Inuit leader John Amagoalik as saying: "Speaking from experience, we found that when we first started talking about land claims in the seventies our own people were an obstacle. They couldn't support something they couldn't understand. We had to spend a lot of time explaining land claims. Our problem was our own people."

2 In addition to the materials indicated in the text, this section was written using information from five anonymous interviews with government and Aboriginal officials directly involved in the negotiation of the ITAs mentioned in this part of the chapter.

3 Although bilateral Final Agreements are the norm, recently they have been accompanied by Tripartite Final Agreements, to which the province is a party, thus potentially complicating the self-government negotiation process.

4 *Haida Nation v. British Columbia (Minister of Forests)* [2004] 3 S.C.R. 511; *Taku River Tlingit First Nation v. British Columbia* [2004] 3 S.C.R. 550.

Bibliography

Primary Sources and Government Documents

Bi-Lateral Agreement between the Kaska and the Yukon Government. 2003. Whitehorse, YT.

Council for Yukon First Nations. N.d. *Yukon Land Claims: Yesterday to Tomorrow*. Whitehorse: Council for Yukon First Nations.

Department of Indian Affairs and Northern Development (DIAND) 2002. *A Strong Future for All: Settling Yukon Land Claims*. Ottawa: Minister of Indian Affairs and Northern Development Canada.

Department of Indian Affairs and Northern Development (DIAND). 1990. *Background Paper: The Comprehensive Land Claim Negotiations of the Labrador Inuit, the Government of Newfoundland and Labrador, and the Government of Canada*. Ottawa: DIAND.

Executive Council. 1997. *Backgrounder #2: Land Claims Backgrounder*. St John's: Executive Council of Newfoundland and Labrador, 5 November. Available at http://www.releases.gov.nl.ca/releases.

First Nations Land Advisory Board. 2008. *Annual Report 2006–2007*. Kanata: First Nations Land Management Resource Centre.

Gingell, Judy. 2006. "Bios – Judy Gingell, President and CEO, Kwanlin Development Corp." Kwanlin Dün First Nation website: http://www.kwanlindun.com.

Government of Newfoundland and Labrador. 2006. "Newfoundland and Labrador will lead Lower Churchill development." *News Releases*, 8 May. Online at http://www.releases.gov.nl.ca/releases.

Indian and Northern Affairs Canada (INAC). 2007. "Community Wellbeing Index." *First Nation Profiles*.

Indian and Northern Affairs Canada (INAC). 2005. *Backgrounder: Kwanlin Dün First Nation.* Ottawa: INAC. http://www.aadnc-aandc.gc.ca.

Indian and Northern Affairs Canada (INAC). 2004. *Fast Facts: Labrador Innu.* Ottawa: INAC. http://www.aadnc-aandc.gc.ca/irp/irp-Pf_e.html/.

Indian and Northern Affairs Canada (INAC). 2003. *Resolving Aboriginal Claims: A Practical Guide to Canadian Experiences.* Ottawa: INAC.

Indian and Northern Affairs Canada (INAC). 2001. *Labrador Inuit Land Claims Agreement-in-Principle (AIP) in Brief.* Ottawa: Minister of Public Works and Government Services Canada.

Indian and Northern Affairs Canada (INAC). 1998. *Federal Policy for the Settlement of Native Claims.* Ottawa: Minister of Public Works and Government Services Canada.

Indian and Northern Affairs Canada (INAC). 1996. *Innu Nation Claim.* http://www.aadnc-aandc.gc.ca/pr/info/info71_e.html.

Indian and Northern Affairs Canada (INAC). 1995. *Federal Policy Guide: Aboriginal Self-Government.* Ottawa: Minister of Public Works and Government Services Canada.

Indian and Northern Affairs Canada (INAC). Specific Claims Branch. 2006. *Public Information Status Report.* Ottawa: Specific Claims Branch.

Innu Nation. 1998. *Money Doesn't Last, The Land Is Forever.* Sheshatshiu: Innu Nation.

Innu Nation. 1995. *Gathering Voices: Finding Strength to Help Our Children by the Davis Inlet People's Inquiry.* Toronto: Douglas & McIntyre.

Kwanlin Dün First Nation. N.d. *Kwanlin Dün First Nation Constitution.* Whitehorse: Kwanlin Dün First Nation.

Kwanlin Dün First Nation. 2005. "Kwanlin Dün Land Claim Signing Ceremony." Kwanlin Dän Ch'a: A Newsletter for and about the Kwanlin Dün People. Whitehorse: Kwanlin Dün First Nation.

Kwanlin Dün First Nation. 2003. *Back to the River: Celebrating Our Culture.* Whitehorse: Kwanlin Dün First Nation.

Kwanlin Dün First Nation. 1994. *Uncovering the Past.* Whitehorse: Kwanlin Dün First Nation.

Kwanlin Dün First Nation. Ratification Committee. 2004. *Kwanlin Dün Land Claim Agreements: A Summary.* Whitehorse: Kwanlin Dün First Nation.

Kwanlin Dün First Nation Final Agreement. 2004. Ottawa: Minister of Indian Affairs and Northern Development.

Kwanlin Dün First Nation Self-Government Agreement. 2004. Ottawa: Minister of Indian Affairs and Northern Development.

Labrador Inuit Association (LIA). 2004. *Annual Report: 2003–2004.* Nain: Labrador Inuit Association.

Labrador Inuit Land Claims Agreement. 2005. Ottawa: Minister of Indian Affairs and Northern Development.

LegendSeekers Anthropological Research. 2000. *Yukon Government Land Claims Training Manual*. LegendSeekers Anthropological Research.

McIntyre, Norman. 2006. *Auditors' Report for Ross River Dena Council, 2005–2006*. Available online at http://ainc-inac.gc.ca.

McLean, Ernest. 2001 *Speaking Notes for Minister of Labrador and Aboriginal Affairs Ernest McLean to the Meeting of Newfoundland and Labrador RED Boards*. Happy Valley–Goose Bay, NL, 12 October. Available at http://www .releases.gov.nl.ca/releases.

Ministry of Aboriginal Relations and Reconciliation. 2010. *Overview: What Are Incremental Treaty Agreements?*

Ministry of Aboriginal Relations and Reconciliation. 2009. *News Release #2009ARR0001-000285, Agreement with Klahoose Builds Economic Opportunities*. Victoria, BC, 5 March.

Nunatsiavut Government. 2006a. "Early History." *Our People*. Nunatsiavut Government.

Nunatsiavut Government. 2006b. "A New Beginning." *Our People*. Nunatsiavut Government.

Nunatsiavut Government. 2006c. "Who We Are." *Our People*. Nunatsiavut Government.

Nunatsiavut Government. 2006d. "Winds of Change." *Our People*. Nunatsiavut Government.

Nunatsiavut Government. 2005. *One Man's Land Claims History: An Interview with Toby Andersen*. Nunatsiavut Government.

O'Brien, Rick. 2006. "Bios – Rick O'Brien Chief, Kwanlin Dün First Nation." Kwanlin Dün First Nation website: http://www.kwanlindun.com.

Office of the Premier. 2008. *News Release #2008OTP0269–001713 First-Ever Incremental Treaty Agreement Reached*. Victoria, British Columbia, 13 November.

Pike, Mark. 2006. *Auditors' Report for Liard First Nation, 2005–2006*.

Rideout, Tom. 2004. "Minister reflects on issues facing Labrador and aboriginal people." News releases: NLIS 4, Labrador and Aboriginal Affairs, 24 August. Available at http://www.releases.gov.nl.ca/releases.

Royal Commission on Aboriginal Peoples (RCAP). 1996. *Report of the Royal Commission on Aboriginal Peoples*. Ottawa: Minister of Supply and Services Canada.

Statistics Canada. 2001. *2001 Census Aboriginal Population Profiles*. Ottawa: Statistics Canada. http://www12.statcan.ca/census-recensement/index-eng.cfm.

Yukon Native Brotherhood. 1973. *Together Today for Our Children Tomorrow*. Whitehorse: Yukon Native Brotherhood.

Secondary Sources

Abele, Frances. 1999. "The Importance of Consent: Indigenous Peoples' Politics in Canada." In James Bickerton and Alain-G. Gagnon, eds, *Canadian Politics*. Peterborough, ON: Broadview Press.

Abele, Frances. 1986. "Conservative Northern Development Policy: A New Broom in an Old Bottleneck?" In Michael J. Prince, ed., *How Ottawa Spends 1986–1987: Tracking the Tories*. London: Methuen Press.

Abele, Frances, and Katherine A. Graham. 1988. "Plus Que ça Change … Northern and Native Policy." In Katherine A. Graham, ed., *How Ottawa Spends 1988–1989: The Conservatives Heading into the Stretch*. Ottawa: Carleton University Press.

Abele, Frances, and Michael J. Prince. 2003. "Aboriginal Governance and Canadian Federalism: A To-Do List for Canada." In François Rocher and Miriam Smith, eds, *New Trends in Canadian Federalism*. Peterborough, ON: Broadview Press.

Abele, Frances, Katherine A. Graham, and Allan Maslove. 2000. "Negotiating Canada: Changes in Aboriginal Policy over the Last Thirty Years." In Leslie A. Pal, ed., *How Ottawa Spends 1999–2000*. Oxford University Press.

Alcantara, Christopher. 2010. "Indigenous Contentious Collective Action in Canada: The Labrador Innu and Their Occupation of the Goose Bay Military Air Base." *Canadian Journal of Native Studies* 30 (1): 21–43.

Alcantara, Christopher. 2009. "Old Wine in New Bottles? Instrumental Policy Learning and the Evolution of the Certainty Provision in Comprehensive Land Claims Agreements." *Canadian Public Policy* 35 (3): 325–41. http://dx.doi.org/10.3138/cpp.35.3.325.

Alcantara, Christopher. 2008. "Aboriginal Policy Reform and the Subsidiarity Principle: A Case Study of the Division of Matrimonial Real Property on Canadian Indian Reserves." *Canadian Public Administration* 51 (2): 317–33. http://dx.doi.org/10.1111/j.1754-7121.2008.00020.x.

Alcantara, Christopher. 2007a. "Explaining Aboriginal Treaty Negotiation Outcomes in Canada: The Cases of the Inuit and the Innu in Labrador." *Canadian Journal of Political Science* 40 (1): 185–207. http://dx.doi.org/10.1017/S0008423907070060.

Alcantara, Christopher. 2007b. "Reduce Transaction Costs? Yes. Strengthen Property Rights? Maybe. The First Nations Land Management Act and

Economic Development on Canadian Indian Reserves." *Public Choice* 132 (3–4): 421–32. http://dx.doi.org/10.1007/s11127-007-9168-7.

Alcantara, Christopher, and Greg Whitfield. 2010. "Aboriginal Self-Government through Constitutional Design: A Survey of Fourteen Aboriginal Constitutions in Canada." *Journal of Canadian Studies / Revue d'Études Canadiennes* 44 (2): 122–45.

Alfred, Taiaiake. 2008. *Peace, Power, Righteousness: An Indigenous Manifesto*. 2nd ed. Toronto: Oxford University Press.

Alfred, Taiaike. 2005. *Wasáse: Indigenous Pathways of Action and Freedom*. Peterborough: ON: Broadview Press.

Andersen, Toby. 2001. *In Directions North: Labrador in the New Century*. Ed. Martha Macdonald. Happy Valley–Goose Bay: Labrador Institute.

Andersen, William, III. 1990. *Labrador in the '90s*. Happy Valley–Goose Bay: Labrador Institute.

Angus, Murray. 1992. "Comprehensive Claims: One Step Forward, Two Steps Back." In Diane Engelstad and John Bird, eds, *Nation to Nation: Aboriginal Sovereignty and the Future of Canada*. Toronto: Anansi.

Asch, Michael. 1999. "From *Calder* to *Van der Peet*: Aboriginal Rights and Canadian Law, 1973–96." In Paul Havemann, ed., *Indigenous Peoples' Rights in Australia, Canada, and New Zealand*. New York: Oxford University Press.

Asch, Michael, and Norman Zlotkin. 1997. "Affirming Aboriginal Title: A New Basis for Comprehensive Claims Negotiations." In Michael Asch, ed., *Aboriginal and Treaty Rights in Canada: Essays on Law, Equality, and Respect for Difference*. Vancouver: UBC Press.

Ashini, Napes. 1992. "Nitassinan: Caribou and F-16s." In Diane Engelstad and John Bird, eds, *Nation to Nation: Aboriginal Sovereignty and the Future of Canada*. Toronto: Anansi.

Backhouse, Catherine, and Donald McRae. 2002. *Canadian Human Rights Commission on the Treatment of the Innu of Labrador by the Government of Canada*. Ottawa: Canadian Human Rights Commission, 26 March.

Baikie, Maureen. 1990. "Perspectives on the Health of the Labrador Inuit." *Northern Perspectives* 18 (2) (March–April).

Bakvis, Herman. 2001. "Prime Minister and Cabinet in Canada: An Autocracy in Need of Reform?" *Journal of Canadian Studies / Revue d'Études Canadiennes*. (Winter) 35 (4): 60–79.

Belanger, Yale, and David Newhouse. 2008. "Reconciling Solitudes: A Critical Analysis of the Self-Government Ideal." In Yale D. Belanger, ed., *Aboriginal Self-Government in Canada: Current Trends and Issues*. Saskatoon: Purich Publishing.

Blackburn, Carole. 2005. "Searching for Guarantees in the Midst of Uncertainty: Negotiating Aboriginal Rights and Title in British Columbia." *American Anthropologist* 107 (4): 586–96. http://dx.doi.org/10.1525/aa.2005.107.4.586.

Borlase, Tim. 1993. *The Labrador Inuit*. Happy Valley–Goose Bay: Labrador East Integrated School Board.

Cameron, Kirk, and Graham Gomme. 1991. *The Yukon's Constitutional Foundations. Volume II: A Compendium of Documents Relating to the Constitutional Development of the Yukon Territory*. Whitehorse: Northern Directories Ltd.

Cameron, Kirk, and Graham White. 1995. *Northern Governments in Transition: Political and Constitutional Development in the Yukon, Nunavut, and the Western Northwest Territories*. Montreal: Institute for Research on Public Policy.

Chartrand, Larry. 2008. "We Rise Again: Métis Traditional Governance and the Claim to Métis Self-Government." In Yale D. Belanger, ed., *Aboriginal Self-Government in Canada: Current Trends and Issues*. Saskatoon: Purich Publishing.

Coates, Ken. 1991. *Best Left as Indians: Native–White Relations in the Yukon Territory, 1840–1973*. Montreal, Kingston: McGill-Queen's University Press.

Coates, Ken, ed. 1992. *Aboriginal Land Claims in Canada: A Regional Perspective*. Toronto: Copp Clark Pitman.

Coates, Ken, and W.R. Morrison. 2008. "From Panacea to Reality: The Practicalities of Canadian Aboriginal Self-Government Arrangements." In Yale D. Belanger, ed., *Aboriginal Self-Government in Canada: Current Trends and Issues*. Saskatoon: Purich Publishing.

Coates, Ken, and Judith Powell. 1989. *The Modern North: People, Politics and the Rejection of Colonialism*. Toronto: James Lorimer and Co.

Cornell, Stephen, and Joseph P. Kalt. 1992. "Reloading the Dice: Improving the Chances of Economic Development on American Indian Reservations." In S. Cornell and J. Kalt, eds, *What Can Tribes Do? Strategies and Institutions in American Indian Economic Development*. Los Angeles: University of California at Los Angeles, American Indian Studies Center.

Costa, Ravi de. 2003. "Treaties in British Columbia: The Search for a New Relationship." *International Journal of Canadian Studies* 27.

Crowe, Keith J. 1991. *A History of the Original Peoples of Northern Canada*. Montreal, Kingston: McGill-Queen's University Press.

Dacks, Gurston. 2002. "British Columbia after the *Delgamuukw* Decision: Land Claims and Other Processes." *Canadian Public Policy* 28 (2): 239–55. http://dx.doi.org/10.2307/3552327.

Dacks, Gurston. 1981. *A Choice of Futures: Politics in the Canadian North*. Toronto: Methuen.

Dewar, Barry. 2009. "Nunavut and the Nunavut Land Claims Agreement – An Unresolved Relationship." *Policy Options* (July–August) 30 (7): 74–9.

Diamond, Billy. 1985. "Aboriginal Rights: The James Bay Experience." In Menno Boldt, J. Anthony Long, and Leroy Little Bear, eds, *The Quest for Justice: Aboriginal Peoples and Aboriginal Rights.* Toronto: University of Toronto Press.

Dorais, Louis-Jacques. 2002. "Inuit." In Paul Robert Magocsi, ed., *Aboriginal Peoples of Canada.* Toronto: University of Toronto Press.

Dyck, Rand. 1996. *Provincial Politics in Canada: Towards the Turn of the Century.* Scarborough: Prentice Hall Canada Inc.

Encarnacion, Omar G. 2000. "Beyond Transitions: The Politics of Democratic Consolidation." *Comparative Politics* 32 (4): 479–97.

Feit, Harvey A. 1980. "Negotiating Recognition of Aboriginal Rights: History, Strategies and Reactions to the James Bay and Northern Quebec Agreement." *Canadian Journal of Anthropology* 1 (2): 159–72.

Fenge, Terry, and Paul Quassa. 2009. "Negotiating and Implementing the Nunavut Land Claims Agreement." *Policy Options* (July–August) 30 (7): 80–6.

Flanagan, Tom, Christopher Alcantara, and Andre Le Dressay. 2010. *Beyond the Indian Act: Restoring Aboriginal Property Rights.* Montreal, Kingston: McGill-Queen's University Press.

Frideres, James S. 1986. "Native Claims and Settlement in Yukon." In Rick Ponting, ed., Arduous Journey: Canadian Indians and Decolonization, 284–301. Toronto: McClelland & Stewart.

Graham, Katherine A. 1987. "Indian Policy and the Tories: Cleaning Up after the Buffalo Jump." In Michael J. Prince, ed., How Ottawa Spends 1987–1988: Restraining the State. Toronto: Methuen Press.

Hall, Peter A. and Rosemary Taylor. 1996. "Political Science and the Three New Institutionalisms." *Political Studies* 44 (5):936–57. http://dx.doi.org/10.1111/j.1467-9248.1996.tb00343.x

Hanson, Stephen and Jeffrey Kopstein. 2005. "Regime Type and Diffusion in Comparative Politics Methodology." *Canadian Journal of Political Science* 38 (1): 69–99.

Haysom, Veryan. 1990. "Labrador Inuit Land Claims: Aboriginal Rights and Interests v. Federal and Provincial Responsibilities and Authorities." *Northern Perspectives* 18 (2).

Henderson, Ailsa. 2008. "Self-Government in Nunavut." In Yale D. Belanger, ed., *Aboriginal Self-Government in Canada: Current Trends and Issues.* Saskatoon: Purich Publishing.

Henriksen, Georg. 1981. "Davis Inlet, Labrador." In June Helm, ed., *Handbook of North American Indians: Volume 6, Subarctic.* Washington: Smithsonian Institution.

Hicks, Jack, and Graham White. 2000. "Nunavut: Inuit Self-Determination through a Land Claim and Public Government?" In Jens Dahl, Jack Hicks, and Peter Jull, eds, *Inuit Regain Control of Their Lands and Their Lives.* Copenhagen: International Work Group for Indigenous Affairs.

Honigmann, John Joseph. 1981. "Kaska." In June Helm, ed., *Handbook of North American Indians: Volume 6, Subarctic.* Washington: Smithsonian Institution.

Honigmann, John Joseph. 1964. *The Kaska Indians: An Ethnographic Reconstruction.* Whitehorse: Human Relations Area Files Press.

Innes, Robert Alexander, and Terrence Ross Pelletier. 2008. "Cowesses First Nation: Self-Government, Nation Building, and Treaty Land Entitlement." In Yale D. Belanger, ed., *Aboriginal Self-Government in Canada: Current Trends and Issues.* Saskatoon: Purich Publishing.

Irlbacher-Fox, Stephanie. 2009. *Finding Dahshaa: Self-Government, Social Suffering, and Aboriginal Policy in Canada.* Vancouver: UBC Press.

Isaac, Thomas. 2005. "First Nations Land Management Act and Third Party Interests." *Alberta Law Review* 42: 1047–60.

Jack, Bart. 1990. *Labrador in the '90s.* Happy Valley–Goose Bay: Labrador Institute.

Kam, Christopher. 2000. "Not Just Parliamentary 'Cowboys and Indians': Ministerial Responsibility and Bureaucratic Drift." *Governance: An International Journal of Policy, Administration and Institutions* 13 (3): 365–92. http://dx.doi.org/10.1111/0952-1895.00138.

Knill, Christoph, and Andrea Lenschow. 2001. "Seek and Ye Shall Find! Linking Different Perspectives on Institutional Change." *Comparative Political Studies* 34 (2): 187–215. http://dx.doi.org/10.1177/0010414001034002003.

Kulchyski, Peter. 2005. *Like the Sound of a Drum: Aboriginal Cultural Politics in Denendeh and Nunavut.* University of Manitoba Press.

Lush, Tom. 2001. "Speaking Notes for the Minister of Intergovernmental Affairs and Government House Leader." In Martha Macdonald, ed., *Directions North: Labrador in the New Century.* Happy Valley–Goose Bay: Labrador Institute.

Lusztig, Michael. 1994. "Constitutional Paralysis: Why Canadian Constitutional Initiatives Are Doomed to Fail." *Canadian Journal of Political Science* 27 (4): 747–71. http://dx.doi.org/10.1017/S0008423900022010.

Macklem, Patrick. 2001. *Indigenous Difference and the Constitution of Canada.* Toronto: University of Toronto Press.

Macklem, Patrick, and Roger Townshend. 1992. "Resorting to Court: Can the Judiciary Deliver Justice for First Nations?" In Diane Engelstad and John Bird, eds, *Nation to Nation: Aboriginal Sovereignty and the Future of Canada.* Toronto: Anansi.

Matthews, Danielle, et al. 2006. "Innu of Labrador." Virtual Museum of Labrador website: http://www.labradorvirtualmuseum.ca.

McClellan, Catharine. 1987. *Part of the Land, Part of the Water: A History of the Yukon Indians*. Vancouver, Toronto: Douglas & McIntyre.

McClellan, Catherine. 1981. "Tutchone." In June Helm, ed., *Handbook of North American Indians: Volume 6, Subarctic*. Washington: Smithsonian Institution.

McCormick, Floyd. 2001. "Still Frontier, Always Homeland: Yukon Politics in the Year 2000." In Keith Brownsey and Michael Howlett, eds, *The Provincial State in Canada: Politics in the Provinces and Territories*. Peterborough, ON: Broadview Press.

McMillan, Alan D., and Eldon Yellowhorn. 2004. *First Peoples in Canada*. Toronto: Douglas & McIntyre.

McPherson, Robert. 2003. *New Owners: Minerals and Inuit Land Claims in Their Own Land*. Calgary: University of Calgary Press.

Miller, J.R. 2009. *Compact, Contract, Covenant: Aboriginal Treaty-Making in Canada*. Toronto: University of Toronto Press.

Miller, J.R. 2000. *Skyscrapers Hide the Heavens: A History of Indian–White Relations in Canada*. Toronto: University of Toronto Press.

Mitchell, Marybelle. 1996. *From Talking Chiefs to a Native Corporate Elite: The Birth of Class and Nationalism among Canadian Inuit*. Montreal, Kingston: McGill-Queen's University Press.

Molloy, Tom. 2000. *The World Is Our Witness: The Historic Journey of the Nisga'a into Canada*. Calgary: Fifth House Publishers.

Monture-Angus, Patricia A. 1999. *Journeying Forward: Dreaming First Nations*. Black Point, NS: Fernwood Press.

Munck, Gerardo. 1994. "Democratic Transitions in Comparative Perspective." *Comparative Politics* 26 (3): 355–75. http://dx.doi.org/10.2307/422116.

Nadasdy, Paul. 2003. *Hunters and Bureaucrats: Power, Knowledge, and Aboriginal–State Relations in the Southwest Yukon*. Vancouver: UBC Press.

North, Douglass. 1990. *Institutions, Institutional Change and Economic Performance*. Cambridge: Cambridge University Press.

Papillon, Martin. 2008. "Aboriginal Quality of Life Under a Modern Treaty." *IRPP Choices* 14 (9): 1–26.

Penashue, Peter. 1992. "Nitassinan: Nation to Nation." In Diane Engelstad and John Bird, eds, *Nation to Nation: Aboriginal Sovereignty and the Future of Canada*. Toronto: Anansi.

Penikett, Tony. 2006. *Reconciliation: First Nations Treaty Making in British Columbia*. Vancouver: Douglas & McArthur.

Rueschemeyer, Dietrich, John Stephens, and Evelyn Huber Stephens. 1992. *Capitalist Development and Democracy*. Chicago: University of Chicago Press.

Rynard, Paul. 2001. "Ally or Colonizer?: The Federal State, the Cree Nation, and the James Bay Agreement." *Journal of Canadian Studies / Revue d'Études Canadiennes* 36 (2): 8–47.

Rynard, Paul. 2000. "Welcome In, but Check Your Rights at the Door": The James Bay and Nisga'a Agreements in Canada." *Canadian Journal of Political Science* 33 (2): 211–43.

Salée, Daniel. 2006. "Quality of Life of Aboriginal People in Canada: An Analysis of Current Research." *IRPP Choices* 12 (6): 1–38.

Samson, Colin. 2003. *A Way of Life That Does Not Exist: Canada and the Extinguishment of the Innu*. St John's: Institute of Social and Economic Research.

Samson, Colin, James Wilson, and Jonathan Mazower. 1999. *Canada's Tibet: The Killing of the Innu*. Survival International.

Savoie, Donald. 1999. *Governing from the Centre: The Concentration of Power in Canadian Politics*. Toronto: University of Toronto Press.

Scholtz, Christa. 2006. *Negotiating Claims: The Emergence of Indigenous Land Claim Negotiation Policies in Australia, Canada, New Zealand, and the United States*. New York: Routledge.

Shapiro, Ian, and Donald Green. 1996. *Pathologies of Rational Choice Theory: A Critique of Applications in Political Science*. New Haven, CT: Yale University Press.

Sharp, Robert. 1976. *The Impact of Anvil Mine on Ross River: Presentation to the Berger Commission Hearings, May 7, 1976*. Whitehorse: Yukon Archives.

Shepsle, Kenneth A. 1989. "Studying Institutions: Some Lessons from the Rational Choice Approach." *Journal of Theoretical Politics* 1 (2): 131–47. http://dx.doi.org/10.1177/0951692889001002002.

Simeon, Richard. 2006. *Federal-Provincial Diplomacy: The Making of Recent Policy in Canada*. Toronto: University of Toronto Press.

Slowey, Gabrielle. 2008. "Unfinished Business: Self-government and the James Bay Northern Quebec Agreement Thirty Years Later." In Yale D. Belanger, ed., *Aboriginal Self-Government in Canada: Current Trends and Issues*. Saskatoon: Purich Publishing.

Summers, Valerie A. 2001. "Between a Rock and a Hard Place: Regime Change in Newfoundland." In Keith Brownsey and Michael Howlett, eds, *The Provincial State in Canada: Politics in the Provinces and Territories*. Peterborough: Broadview Press.

Thomas, Paul G. 1999. "The Role of Central Agencies: Making a Mesh of Things." In James Bickerton and Alain-G. Gagnon, eds, *Canadian Politics*. Peterborough: Broadview Press.

Tsebelis, George. 2002. *Veto Players: How Political Institutions Work*. Princeton, NJ: Princeton University Press.

Tully, James. 2001. "Reconsidering the B.C. Treaty Process." In *Speaking Truth to Power: A Treaty Forum*. Ottawa: Law Commission of Canada.

Wadden, Marie. 1991. *Nitassinan: The Innu Struggle to Reclaim Their Homeland*. Toronto: Douglas & McIntyre.

White, Graham. 2003. "And Now for Something Completely Northern: Institutions of Governance in the Territorial North." In Robert B. Anderson and Robert B. Bone, eds, *In Natural Resources and Aboriginal Peoples in Canada*. Concord, ON: Captus Press.

White, Graham. 2002a. "Politics and Government in the Territorial North: Familiar and Exotic." In *The CRIC Papers. The Canadian North: Embracing Change*. Ottawa: CRIC.

White, Graham. 2002b. "Treaty Federalism in Northern Canada: Aboriginal-Government Land Claims Boards." *Publius: The Journal of Federalism* 32 (3): 89–114. http://dx.doi.org/10.1093/oxfordjournals.pubjof.a004961.

Widdowson, Frances, and Albert Howard. 2008. *Disrobing the Aboriginal Industry: The Deception behind Indigenous Cultural Preservation*. Montreal, Kingston: Montreal-Queen's University Press.

Media Sources

Brethour, Patrick. 2007. "Band to withdraw from treaty talks." *Globe and Mail*, 31 March: A2.

Brown, Sarah Elizabeth. 2003. "Suit filed as chief's sentencing delayed." *Whitehorse Daily Star Online*, 10 October. www.whitehorsestar.com.

Canadian Broadcasting Corporation (CBC). 2008. "Innu hydro deal will be hard to sell, former leader claims." *CBC Online*, 29 September. www.cbc.ca.

Canadian Broadcasting Corporation (CBC). 2006a. "Vandalism shuts down Innu Nation office." *CBC Online*, 12 January. www.cbc.ca.

Canadian Broadcasting Corporation (CBC). 2006b. "Protest prompts Liard chief to hold AGM." *CBC Online*, 19 April. www.cbc.ca.

Canadian Broadcasting Corporation (CBC). 2006c. "Election call illegal: Innu Nation president." *CBC Online*, 20 June. www.cbc.ca.

Canadian Broadcasting Corporation (CBC). 2006d. "Take over Voisey's trust revenues, Innu man asks court." *CBC Online*, 14 November. www.cbc.ca.

Canadian Broadcasting Corporation (CBC). 2006e. "Receipts for missing funds were stolen: Natuashish chief." *CBC Online*, 27 November. www.cbc.ca.

Canadian Broadcasting Corporation (CBC). 2005a. "The Innu of Labrador: From Davis Inlet to Natuashish." *CBC Online*, 14 February. www.cbc.ca.

Canadian Broadcasting Corporation (CBC). 2005b. "Labrador Innu band defends handling of funds." *CBC Online*, 1 March. www.cbc.ca.

Canadian Broadcasting Corporation (CBC). 2005c. "Alcohol abuse impairs Innu education, report says." *CBC Online,* 7 July. www.cbc.ca.

Canadian Broadcasting Corporation (CBC). 2004. "Bottles bought ballots in Innu election, critics charge." *CBC Online,* 7 October. www.cbc.ca.

Canadian Broadcasting Corporation (CBC). 2002. "Minister will have to wait for Kaska: Negotiator." *CBC Online,* 1 August. www.cbc.ca.

Canadian Broadcasting Corporation (CBC). 2000a. "Innu and loggers to meet." *CBC Online,* 27 July. www.cbc.ca.

Canadian Broadcasting Corporation (CBC). 2000b. "Innu take on the military over test flights." *CBC Online,* 10 November. www.cbc.ca.

Cayo, Don. 2006. "The treaty process needs incentives." *Vancouver Sun,* 1 December.

Curry, Bill. 2007. "Governments urged to end native blockade." *Globe and Mail,* 30 August: A7.

Huggard, Eric. 1987. "The Yukon Indian land claim." *Whitehorse Daily Star,* August.

McNeely, Sean. 1998. "Meeting was extremely productive." *Whitehorse Daily Star Online,* 6 October. www.whitehorsestar.com.

Northern Native Broadcasting Yukon. 1998. "Kwanlin Dün History." *NEDAA Video,* Season 12, show no. 16.

Northern Native Broadcasting Yukon. 1997. "Land Claims '97: Champagne-Aishihik, Kwanlin Dün, Little Salmon-Carmacks." *NEDAA Video,* Season 11, show no. 19.

Northern Native Broadcasting Yukon. 1996. *NEDAA Video,* Season 10, show no. 9.

O'Grady, Candice. 2005. "First nation takes question to court." *Whitehorse Daily Star Online,* 18 August. www.whitehorsestar.com.

Parker, Brigitte D. 1999a. "Councillors demand resignation." *Whitehorse Daily Star Online,* 25 January. www.whitehorsestar.com.

Parker, Brigitte D. 1999b. "Business as Usual." *Whitehorse Daily Star Online,* 27 January. www.whitehorsestar.com.

Raybould, Tim. 2007. "Just who needs treaties?" *Globe and Mail,* 4 April.

Small, Jason. 2004. "First nation takes step back from CYFN." *Whitehorse Daily Star Online.* 17 September. www.whitehorsestar.com.

Small, Jason. 2003. "Tearful O'Brien wins AFN vice-chief post." *Whitehorse Daily Star Online,* 9 July. www.whitehorsestar.com.

Small, Jason. 2002a. "Historic new Yukon Act approved." *Whitehorse Daily Star Online,* 27 March. www.whitehorsestar.com.

Small, Jason. 2002b. "Supreme Court of Canada rules against Kaska." *Whitehorse Daily Star Online,* 21 June. www.whitehorsestar.com.

Small, Jason. 2002c. "Kaska first nations will review claims package." *White-horse Daily Star Online*, 27 June. www.whitehorsestar.com.

Small, Jason. 2002d. "Kaska optimistic about Fentie's regime." *Whitehorse Daily Star Website*, 9 December. www.whitehorsestar.com.

Small, Jason. 2001a. "Claims may reach fruition by March." *Whitehorse Daily Star Online*, 14 August. www.whitehorsestar.com.

Small, Jason. 2001b. "Transfer of powers delayed again." *Whitehorse Daily Star Online*, 25 September. www.whitehorsestar.com.

Tobin, Chuck. 2005a. "It is the beginning of a new future." *Whitehorse Daily Star Online*, 21 February. www.whitehorsestar.com.

Tobin, Chuck. 2005b. "We have to operate on crumbs, chief says." *Whitehorse Daily Star Online*, 15 March. www.whitehorsestar.com.

Tobin, Chuck. 2005c. "Thirty-two years of land claim talks end." *Whitehorse Daily Star Online*, 1 April. www.whitehorsestar.com.

Tobin, Chuck. 2004a. "They want to put Daniel away, leader says." *Whitehorse Daily Star Online*, 17 March. www.whitehorsestar.com.

Tobin, Chuck. 2004b. "Land claim vote put off to the fall." *Whitehorse Daily Star Online*, 11 May. www.whitehorsestar.com.

Tobin, Chuck. 2003a. "Nault weighing Kaska, YTG proposal." *Whitehorse Daily Star Online*, 14 January. www.whitehorsestar.com.

Tobin, Chuck. 2003b. "Kaska want to be consulted about mining." *Whitehorse Daily Star Online*, 16 January. www.whitehorsestar.com.

Tobin, Chuck. 2003c. "YTG won't intervene in landmark court battle." *White-horse Daily Star Online*, 10 April. www.whitehorsestar.com.

Tobin, Chuck. 2002a. "Eleventh-hour claim deals signed." *Whitehorse Daily Star Online*, 1 April 1. www.whitehorsestar.com.

Tobin, Chuck. 2002b. "Document summarizes terms of Kwanlin Dün land claim." *Whitehorse Daily Star Online*, 11 December. www.whitehorsestar.com.

Tobin, Chuck. 1999a. "Jack and Joe sit down together." *Whitehorse Daily Star Online*, 11 January. www.whitehorsestar.com.

Tobin, Chuck. 1999b. "Chief makes surprise bid to keep job." *Whitehorse Daily Star Online*, 9 March. www.whitehorsestar.com.

Tobin, Chuck. 1999c. "Kwanlin Dün chief suffers massive defeat." *Whitehorse Daily Star Online*, 23 March. www.whitehorsestar.com.

Waddell, Stephanie. 2003. "City is closer to selling waterfront area to YTG." *Whitehorse Daily Star Online*, 18 June. www.whitehorsestar.com.

Waddell, Stephanie. 2001. "Premier reviews year for communities." *Whitehorse Daily Star Online*, 9 May. www.whitehorsestar.com.

Whitehorse Daily Star Staff Writers. 2001. "Kaska put cases in abeyance." *Whitehorse Daily Star Online*, 12 April. www.whitehorsestar.com.

Whitehorse Daily Star Staff Writers. 1998a. "Councillors oppose separation process." *Whitehorse Daily Star Online*, 15 January. www.whitehorsestar.com.
Whitehorse Daily Star Staff Writers. 1998b. "Chief Says Separation Will Happen." *Whitehorse Daily Star Online*, 23 January. www.whitehorsestar.com.

Interviews

Andersen, Chesley. 2006. Former LIA negotiator and current secretary to the Executive Council for the Nunatsiavut Government. Personal interview. Makkovik, Labrador, 24 February.
Andersen, Tony. 2006. Former LIA vice-president and current first minister, Department of Nunatsiavut Affairs. Personal interview. Nain, Labrador, 20 February.
Andersen, William, III. 2006. Former LIA president and current Nunatsiavut Government president. Personal interview, Nain, Labrador, 23 February.
Andrew, Ben. 2006. Innu Nation official and negotiator. Personal interview. Sheshatshiu, Labrador, 13 February.
Armour, Karyn. 2006. Assistant deputy minister for YT Land Claims Secretariat. Personal interview. Whitehorse, YT, 24 October.
Ashini, John-Pierre. 2006. Innu Nation official. Personal interview. Sheshatshiu, Labrador, 13 February.
Barbour, William. 2006. Former LIA president. Personal interview. Nain, Labrador, 21 February.
Barichello, Norm. 2006. Land claims adviser to the Kaska on issues such as fish and wildlife, special management areas, culture and heritage, and forestry. Personal interview. Whitehorse, YT, 26 October.
Beaudoin, Tom. 2006. Land claims director, Kwanlin Dun First Nation. Personal interview. Whitehorse, YT, 26 October.
Benuen, Damien. 2006. Innu Nation vice-president. Personal interview. Natuashish, Labrador, 17 February.
Bourassa, Ernie. 2006. Former mayor of the City of Whitehorse, 2000–6. Personal interview. Whitehorse, YT, 23 October.
Brown, Keith. 2006. Former legal counsel for Kwanlin Dün and Kaska First Nations. Personal interview. Vancouver, BC, 20 October.
Carter, Ruby. 2006. Senior provincial negotiator for the Inuit file. Personal interview. St John's, NL, 27 February.
Dick, Hammond. 2006. Kaska Tribal Council hereditary chief. Personal interview. Watson Lake, YT, 31 October.
Dixon, Dave. 2006. Liard First Nation band councillor. Personal interview. Watson Lake, YT, 31 October.

Flynn, Dermot. 2006. Chief YT negotiator for the Kaska and Kwanlin Dün files, 1983–present. Personal interview. Whitehorse, YT, 24 October.

Gour, Christiane. 2006. "Registered Indian population by sex and residence." First Nations and Northern Statistics section, Indian and Northern Affairs Canada (email correspondence).

Hanson, Elizabeth. 2006. Former regional director general for INAC in Whitehorse. Personal interview. Whitehorse, YT, 25 October.

Hawco, Ray. 2006. Former provincial chief negotiator for Newfoundland and Labrador. Personal interview. St John's, NL, 26 February.

Haysom, Veryan. 2006. LIA negotiator. Telephone interview. Halifax, NS, 2 March.

Hibbs, Mina Campbell. 2006. LIA board member. Personal interview. North West River, Labrador, 16 February.

Innes, Larry. 2006. Innu Nation lawyer and negotiator. Telephone interview. Happy Valley–Goose Bay, Labrador, 7 March.

Jararuse, John. 2006. Inuit elder. Personal interview. Nain, Labrador, 23 February.

Joe, Dave. 2006. Former legal counsel for Council of Yukon Indians, negotiator on the Umbrella Final Agreement. Personal interview. Vancouver, BC, 16 October.

King, Anne. 2006. Legal counsel for the federal government, Kwanlin Dün Final Agreement Negotiations, 1991–2004. Personal interview. Whitehorse, YT, 26 October.

Koepke, Tim. 2006. Federal chief negotiator for the Umbrella Final Agreement and the Kaska and Kwanlin Dün files. Personal interview. Vancouver, BC, 18 October.

Mackenzie, Jim. 2006. Former chief federal negotiator for the Inuit file. Telephone interview. Ottawa, 30 April.

Marshall, Harold. 2006. Former senior civil servant for Newfoundland and Labrador. Telephone interview, St John's, NL, 5 March.

McArthur, Doug. 2006. Former deputy minister, YT Land Claims Secretariat, 1989–92. Personal interview. Vancouver, BC, 20 October.

McCullough, Lesley. 2006. Director of research for YT Land Claims Secretariat. Personal interview. Whitehorse, YT, 24 October.

McMillan, Liard. 2006. Liard First Nation chief. Personal interview. Watson Lake, YT, 1 November.

Michel, Ben. 2006. Former Innu negotiator for Sheshatshiu and current Innu Nation president. Telephone interview. Sheshatshiu, Labrador, 24 January.

Mitander, Victor. 2006. Former Council of Yukon Indians negotiator on the Umbrella Final Agreement. Personal interview. Whitehorse, YT, 23 October.

Nui, Mark. 2006. Current Innu Nation negotiator representing Natuashish. Personal interview. Natuashish, Labrador, 17 February.

Nuke, Ponus. 2006. Innu elder. Personal interview. Sheshatshiu, Labrador, 15 February.

Pain, Isabella. 2006. LIA negotiator. Personal interview. Nain, Labrador. 23 February.

Pelley, Bob. 2006. Senior provincial negotiator for the Innu file. Personal interview. St John's, NL, 27 February.

Penikett, Tony. 2006. Former premier of the YT, 1985–92. Personal interview. Vancouver, BC, 18 October.

Poker, Prote. 2006. Former Innu chief of Davis Inlet and current Innu Nation official. Personal interview. Natuashish, Labrador, 17 February.

Porter, Dave. 2006. Kaska chief negotiator. Personal interview. Vancouver, BC, 17 October.

Porter, Dennis. 2006. Kaska elder. Personal interview. Watson Lake, YT, 31 October.

Raider, Ann Maje. 2006. Former chief of Liard First Nation 1992–8. Personal interview. Watson Lake, YT, 1 November.

Rich, Paul. 2006. Former Innu chief of Sheshatshiu. Personal interview. Happy Valley–Goose Bay, Labrador, 16 February.

Riche, Joseph. 2006. Innu negotiator for Sheshatshiu. Personal interview. Sheshatshiu, Labrador, 13 February.

Rowell, Judy. 2006. LIA negotiator. Telephone interview. Nain, Labrador, 6 March.

Samson, Mike. 2006. Former deputy minister of Labrador and Aboriginal Affairs. Telephone interview. St John's, NL, 29 May.

Serson, Scott. 2006. Former deputy minister of INAC. Telephone interview. Ottawa, 24 March.

Shafto, Penny. 2006. Former senior federal negotiator for the Inuit file. Telephone interview. Ottawa, 23 March.

Sterriah, Norman. 2006. Former Ross River Dena council chief and land negotiator. Personal interview. Ross River, YT, 30 October.

Stockdale, Dave. 2006. Whitehorse city councillor, 1983–present. Personal interview. Whitehorse, YT, 23 October.

Van Bibber, Eileen. 2006. Liard First Nation elder and former employee of the Liard First Nation band council. Personal interview. Watson Lake, YT, 2 November.

Walsh, Steve. 2006. Legal counsel to the Kaska Nation. Personal interview. Whitehorse, YT, 22 October.

Warren, Bob. 2006. Former senior provincial negotiator for the Inuit file. Telephone interview. Cornerbrook, NL, 30 March.
Whittington, Michael. 2005. Former senior federal negotiator for the Yukon. Email correspondence. Ottawa, 29 May.

Unpublished Theses and Dissertations

McCormick, Floyd. 1997. "Inherent Aboriginal Rights in Theory and Practice: The Council for Yukon Indians Umbrella Final Agreement." PhD dissertation. University of Alberta.

Index

Kaska language, 115
Kaska Nations, 4, 11–12; acculturation and, 115; "cede, release, and
surrender" by, 24–5, 95–6, 99–
100, 106; drug abuse and, 109–10,
153n15; education in, 109–10; English language and, 26–7; extinguishment and, 24–5, 103, 114;
history of, 78–81; illegal resource
development and, 27–8; litigation
by, 30, 95–7, 105, 152n12; mandate
in, 106, 111–12; representation of,
20; self-government and, 112–13;
sovereignty of, 24–5, 103; taxation
and, 95; transboundary issue and,
95, 99–100, 118; trapping by, 95,
99–100; trust and, 116–17; Umbrella
Final Agreement and, 85–7, 94–101
Kaska Traditional Territory, 24–5
Kaska Tribal Council (KTC), 108–9;
creation of, 20, 80, 94–6; disunity
in, 114
KDFN. See Kwanlin Dün First
Nation
Klahoose First Nation, 127–9
Koepke, Tim, 117
KTC. See Kaska Tribal Council
Kusawa Park, 93
Kwanlin Dün First Nation (KDFN),
4, 86–7; acculturation in, 115;
"cede, release, and surrender" by,
25–6, 92, 102; certainty and, 102;
Council of Yukon First Nations
and, 87; delay and, 67; education
in, 132–3; Final Agreement, 91–4,
105–6, 130; history of, 74–8; illegal economic development and,
27–8; Indian and Northern Affairs
Canada on, 78; litigation by, 104;
protests by, 104; self-government

by, 78, 89; Self-Government Agreement, 130, 132–3; sovereignty and,
25–6, 102; taxation and, 89, 93–4,
151n6; trade with, 74–6; trust and,
116–17; Umbrella Final Agreement
and, 20, 98–9; as understudied, 10–
11; in Whitehorse Indian Band, 77

Labrador, 35, 36, 37
Labrador Innu. See Innu
"The Labrador Innu Comprehensive
Healing Strategy," 142–3
Labrador Inuit. See Inuit
Labrador Inuit Alcohol and Drug
Abuse Program, 64–5
Labrador Inuit Association (LIA), 20,
22, 37–8; education and, 64–5; Our
Footprints Our Everywhere, 41
Labrador Inuit Development Corpo-
ration, 38
Labrador Inuit Final Agreement,
48–51
Labrador Inuit Health Commission,
38
Labrador Inuit Lands, 48–9
Labrador Inuit Settlement Lands,
48–50
land claims secretariat, 19–20
land quantum, 50–1
land selection, 48
land-use competition, 68, 71–2,
117–18
language: Aboriginal, 15; English,
26–7, 36–7, 66; French, 66; inter-
preter, 64–5, 115; Kaska, 115; official
discourse, 7–8, 26–7
leadership, 111–12
Lewes Marsh Habitat Protection
Area, 93
LIA. See Labrador Inuit Association